JavaScript Unit Testing

Your comprehensive and practical guide to efficiently performing and automating JavaScript unit testing

Hazem Saleh

[PACKT] open source✲
PUBLISHING   community experience distilled

BIRMINGHAM - MUMBAI

JavaScript Unit Testing

Copyright © 2013 Packt Publishing

First published: January 2013

Production Reference: 1040113

Published by Packt Publishing Ltd.
Livery Place
35 Livery Street
Birmingham B3 2PB, UK.

ISBN 978-1-78216-062-5

www.packtpub.com

Cover Image by Jasmine Doremus (jasdoremus@gmail.com)

Credits

Author
Hazem Saleh

Reviewer
Allan Lykke Christensen

Acquisition Editor
Jonathan Titmus

Commissioning Editors
Harsha Bharwani

Priyanka Shah

Technical Editors
Hardik Soni

Devdutt Kulkarni

Copy Editors
Brandt D'Mello

Insiya Morbiwala

Alfida Paiva

Project Coordinator
Priya Sharma

Proofreaders
Lawrence A. Herman

Joel Johnson

Indexer
Hemangini Bari

Graphics
Aditi Gajjar

Production Coordinator
Melwyn D'sa

Cover Work
Melwyn D'sa

About the Author

Hazem Saleh has 9 years of experience in JEE and open source technologies. He has worked as a technical consultant for different clients in Europe (Sweden), North America (USA, Canada), South America (Peru), Africa (Egypt), and Asia (Qatar, Kuwait). He is an Apache MyFaces committer, and the founder of many open source projects.

Besides being the co-author of the book *The Definitive Guide to Apache MyFaces and Facelets, Zubin Wadia, Martin Marinschek, Hazem Saleh, Dennis Byrne, Apress* and the author of this book, Hazem is also an author of many technical articles, a developerWorks contributing author, and a technical speaker at both local and international conferences, such as the IBM Regional Technical Exchange, CONFESS, and JavaOne. Hazem is now working for IBM Egypt (Cairo Lab SWG Services) as an Advisory Software Engineer. He is a Web 2.0 subject matter expert and an IBM Certified Expert IT Specialist.

I would like to thank my mother, my father, my brother Mohamed, my sister Omnia, and all my family for endlessly supporting me while writing this book. I would like to thank the love and best friend of my life, my wife Naglaa, for encouraging and supporting me while writing this book. I would like to thank all the people who have done me a favor; I would like to thank Ahmed Fouad, Tamer Mahfouz, my dearest brothers Ali AlKahki and Amr Ali, and every one who has done me any kind of favor.

About the Reviewer

Allan Lykke Christensen is the Director of Interactive Media Management and the Vice President of Danish ICT Management, an international consulting firm with a focus on ICT in developing economies. He is responsible for the daily management of teams in Uganda, Bangladesh, and Denmark. In his daily work, he is also responsible for project planning, initiating, and overall implementation. He has been developing and implementing IT projects for more than 10 years. His expertise covers a wide range; he has developed workflow systems, information systems, e-learning tools, knowledge-management systems, and websites. He has worked as Team Leader on several major European Commission financed ICT projects in various developing economies. He has co-authored the book *The Definitive Guide to Apache MyFaces and Facelets, Apress*, and made countless presentations and training sessions on programming-related topics around the world. Allan is also the Lead Developer of the CONVERGE project, which aims at implementing an open source, editorial content management system for media houses. More information on this can be found at http://www.getconverge.com.

www.PacktPub.com

Support files, eBooks, discount offers and more

You might want to visit www.PacktPub.com for support files and downloads related to your book.

Did you know that Packt offers eBook versions of every book published, with PDF and ePub files available? You can upgrade to the eBook version at www.PacktPub.com and as a print book customer, you are entitled to a discount on the eBook copy. Get in touch with us at service@packtpub.com for more details.

At www.PacktPub.com, you can also read a collection of free technical articles, sign up for a range of free newsletters, and receive exclusive discounts and offers on Packt books and eBooks.

http://PacktLib.PacktPub.com

Do you need instant solutions to your IT questions? PacktLib is Packt's online digital book library. Here, you can access, read and search across Packt's entire library of books.

Why Subscribe?

- Fully searchable across every book published by Packt
- Copy and paste, print, and bookmark content
- On demand and accessible via web browser

Free Access for Packt account holders

If you have an account with Packt at www.PacktPub.com, you can use this to access PacktLib today and view nine entirely free books. Simply use your login credentials for immediate access.

Table of Contents

Preface

One of the biggest challenges of many web applications is being supported by different browsers with different versions. JavaScript code that runs on the Safari browser will not necessarily run correctly on Internet Explorer (IE), Firefox, or Google chrome browsers. This challenge is caused by the lack of unit testing of the JavaScript code that has lived in the web application from day one. Without unit testing the JavaScript code, more money will have to be spent for testing and retesting the application's web pages after deciding to upgrade to current, supported browsers (or after updating the JavaScript code of the web pages with non-trivial features).

The *JavaScript Unit Testing* book is a comprehensive practical guide that illustrates in detail how to efficiently create and automate JavaScript tests for web applications using popular, JavaScript unit testing frameworks, such as Jasmine, YUI Test, QUnit, and JsTestDriver.

This book explains the concept of JavaScript unit testing and explores the bits of an interactive Ajax web application (the weather application). Throughout the book, the JavaScript part of the weather application is tested using different JavaScript unit testing frameworks. The book illustrates how to generate test and code coverage reports of developed JavaScript tests. It also explains how to automate the running of JavaScript tests from build and continuous integration tools. The book shows how to integrate different JavaScript unit testing frameworks with each other in order to test web applications in the most efficient way.

What this book covers

Chapter 1, Unit Testing JavaScript Applications, helps you understand what unit testing is, the requirements of a good unit test, and why unit testing is needed. You will also learn the difference between Test-Driven Development and traditional unit testing. You will understand the complexities of testing JavaScript code, and the requirements of good, JavaScript unit testing tools. In this chapter, we will explore the weather web application's JavaScript section which we will unit test in the next chapters.

Chapter 2, Jasmine, helps you learn what Jasmine is and how to use it for testing synchronous JavaScript code. You will learn how to test asynchronous (Ajax) JavaScript code using the Jasmine Spies, waitsFor, and runs mechanisms. You will learn how to perform mock Ajax testing using Jasmine. You will learn about the various matchers provided by the framework, and how to load HTML fixtures in your Jasmine tests. In this chapter, you will learn how to use Jasmine for testing the weather application's JavaScript section.

Chapter 3, YUI Test, helps you to learn what YUI Test is and how to use this JavaScript unit testing framework for testing synchronous JavaScript code. You will learn how to test asynchronous (Ajax) JavaScript code using the YUI Test's wait and resume mechanisms. You will learn about the various assertions provided by the framework, how to display XML and JSON test reports using framework reporter APIs, and how to generate test reports automatically using the YUI Test Selenium Driver. You will learn how to automate running YUI tests using the YUI Test Selenium Driver, and how to integrate an automation script with build management and continuous integration tools. In this chapter, you will learn how to use YUI Test for testing the weather application's JavaScript section.

Chapter 4, QUnit, helps you to understand what QUnit is and how to use it for testing synchronous JavaScript code. You will learn how to test asynchronous (Ajax) JavaScript code using the QUnit test mechanism and the QUnit asyncTest mechanism. You will also learn the different assertions provided by the framework, and how to develop your own assertion in order to simplify your test code. You will learn how to load HTML fixtures in your QUnit tests. In this chapter, you will learn how to use the framework for testing the weather application's JavaScript section.

Chapter 5, JsTestDriver, helps you to learn what JsTestDriver (JSTD) is, the JSTD architecture, the JSTD configuration, and how to use JSTD for testing synchronous JavaScript code. You will learn how to test asynchronous (Ajax) JavaScript code using the JSTD AsyncTestCase object. You will learn the various assertions provided by the framework, and how to generate test and code coverage reports using the framework's code coverage plugin. You will learn how to use JSTD as a test runner for the other JavaScript unit testing frameworks mentioned in the book, such as

Jasmine and QUnit, in order to enable the execution of the tests of these frameworks from the command-line interface. You will learn how to integrate the tests of JSTD (and the tests of the JavaScript frameworks on top of JSTD) with build and continuous integration tools. You will learn how to work with the JSTD framework in one of the most popular integrated development environments (IDEs) which is Eclipse. In this chapter, you will learn how to use JSTD for testing the weather application's JavaScript section.

What you need for this book

You will need the following software in order to run all of the examples in this book:

- Apache Tomcat 6, which can be found at `http://tomcat.apache.org/download-60.cgi`
- Java Development Kit (JDK) Version 5.0 or later, which can be found at `http://www.oracle.com/technetwork/java/javase/downloads/index.html`
- The Selenium Server version 2.25.0 (for *Chapter 3, YUI Test* only), which can be found at `http://seleniumhq.org/download/`
- Eclipse IDE (for *Chapter 5, JsTestDriver* only), which can be found at `http://www.eclipse.org/downloads/packages/release/indigo/sr2`

Who this book is for

The target audience for this book is developers, designers, and architects of web applications.

Conventions

In this book, you will find a number of styles of text that distinguish between different kinds of information. Here are some examples of these styles, and an explanation of their meaning.

Code words in text are shown as follows: "The `validateLoginForm` function calls the `LoginClient` JavaScript object, which is responsible for validating the login form."

A block of code is set as follows:

```
function validateLoginForm() {
    var loginClient = new weatherapp.LoginClient();
```

```
var loginForm = {
  "userNameField" : "username",
  "passwordField" : "password",
  "userNameMessage" : "usernameMessage",
  "passwordMessage" : "passwordMessage"
};

return loginClient.validateLoginForm(loginForm);
}
```

When we wish to draw your attention to a particular part of a code block, the relevant lines or items are set in bold:

```
<!DOCTYPE html>
<html>
<head>
  <meta charset="utf-8">
  <title>QUnit test runner</title>
  <link rel="stylesheet" href="lib/qunit-1.10.0.css">
</head>
<body>
  <div id="qunit"></div>
  <div id="qunit-fixture"></div>
  <script src="lib/qunit-1.10.0.js"></script>

  ...The test code here...
</body>
</html>
```

Any command line input or output is written as follows:

```
java -jar JsTestDriver-1.3.4.b.jar --port 9876 --browser [firefoxpath],
[iepath],[chromepath]
```

New terms and **important words** are shown in bold. Words that you see on the screen, in menus or dialog boxes, for example, appear in the text like this: "In this application, the user enters his/her name and then clicks on the **Welcome** button."

 Warnings or important notes appear in a box like this.

 Tips and tricks appear like this.

Reader feedback

Feedback from our readers is always welcome. Let us know what you think about this book—what you liked or may have disliked. Reader feedback is important for us to develop titles that you really get the most out of.

To send us general feedback, simply send an e-mail to feedback@packtpub.com, and mention the book title via the subject of your message.

If there is a topic that you have expertise in and you are interested in either writing or contributing to a book, see our author guide at www.packtpub.com/authors.

Customer support

Now that you are the proud owner of a Packt book, we have a number of things to help you to get the most from your purchase.

Downloading the example code

You can download the example code files for all Packt books you have purchased from your account at http://www.PacktPub.com. If you purchased this book elsewhere, you can visit http://www.PacktPub.com/support and register to have the files e-mailed directly to you.

Errata

Although we have taken every care to ensure the accuracy of our content, mistakes do happen. If you find a mistake in one of our books—maybe a mistake in the text or the code—we would be grateful if you would report this to us. By doing so, you can save other readers from frustration and help us improve subsequent versions of this book. If you find any errata, please report them by visiting http://www.packtpub.com/support, selecting your book, clicking on the **errata submission form** link, and entering the details of your errata. Once your errata are verified, your submission will be accepted and the errata will be uploaded on our website, or added to any list of existing errata, under the Errata section of that title. Any existing errata can be viewed by selecting your title from http://www.packtpub.com/support.

Piracy

Piracy of copyright material on the Internet is an ongoing problem across all media. At Packt, we take the protection of our copyright and licenses very seriously. If you come across any illegal copies of our works, in any form, on the Internet, please provide us with the location address or website name immediately so that we can pursue a remedy.

Please contact us at copyright@packtpub.com with a link to the suspected pirated material.

We appreciate your help in protecting our authors, and our ability to bring you valuable content.

Questions

You can contact us at questions@packtpub.com if you are having a problem with any aspect of the book, and we will do our best to address it.

1
Unit Testing JavaScript Applications

Before going into the details of unit testing JavaScript applications, we need to understand first what unit testing is and why we need to unit test our applications. This chapter also shows the complexities of testing JavaScript applications and why it is not as simple as desktop applications. Finally, the chapter illustrates the functionality and the JavaScript code of a sample weather application. We will unit test its JavaScript code in the following chapters of the book.

What unit testing is

Unit testing is not a new concept in the software development world. Thanks to Kent Beck, the concept of unit testing was introduced in **Smalltalk**, then the concept was transferred to many other programming languages, such as C, C++, and Java. The classical definition of unit testing is that it is a piece of code (usually a method) that invokes another piece of code and later checks the correctness of some assumptions.

The definition is technically correct; however, it does not show us how to make a really good unit test. In order to write a good unit test, we need to understand the requirements of a good unit test.

As shown in the following figure, a good unit test should be automated, repeatable, easy to understand, incremental, easy to run, and fast.

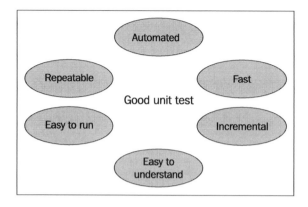

A good unit test should be automated and repeatable, which means that other team members can repeat running the application unit tests for every significant code change automatically. It should also be easy to understand so that other team members can understand what your test means and can continue adding more test cases or updating an existing test case. A good unit test should be incremental; this means that the unit test should be updated if a new relevant defect is detected in the code, which means that this defect will not happen again as long as this unit test is running periodically. Finally, a good unit test should be easy to run; it should run by executing a command or by clicking a button and should not take a long time for execution because fast unit tests can help in increasing the development team's productivity.

So let's go back to the definition and refine it. Unit testing is a piece of code (usually a method) that invokes another piece of code and checks the correctness of some assumptions later. Unit testing should be automated, repeatable, easy to understand, incremental, easy to run, and fast.

Why we need unit testing

Unit testing applications is not something nice to have. It is actually a mandatory activity for having a successful software solutions that can cope with different changes across time with high stability. There is no excuse to skip unit testing of applications even for projects with a tight schedule. The importance of unit testing may not appear in the early stages of the project; however, its advantages are visible in the middle and the final stages of the project, when the code gets complicated, more features are required, and more regression defects appear (defects that appear again after a major code change).

Without unit testing, the integration of the different components in the system becomes complicated. This complexity results from the tracing of the defects of not only the integration between the components but also each "buggy" component. This complicates the life of the developers by making them spend nights in the office in order to meet the schedule.

The number of new defects and the regression defects becomes unmanageable when the code base becomes complicated and unit testing is not available. The developer can resolve a specific defect and, after a set of code changes, this defect can happen again because there is no repeatable test case to ensure that the defect will not happen again.

Having more number of defects per lines of code affects the application's quality badly, and this means that more time has to be spent on testing the application. Bad quality applications have a longer test cycle for each project deployment (or phase), because they have a high probability of having more defects for every code change, which leads to more pressure on the project management, the project developers, and the project testers.

Having good unit testing can be a good reference for the system documentation because it contains the test scenarios of the system use cases. In addition to this, unit testing shows how the system APIs are used, which reflect the current design of the system. This means that unit testing is a powerful basis of code and design refactoring for having more enhancements in the system.

Having good unit testing minimizes the number of regression defects because in good unit testing the system has a repeatable number of test cases for every relevant defect. Having a continuous integration job that runs periodically on the application unit tests will ensure that these defects will not happen again, because if a specific defect appears again due to a change in the application code, then the developer will be notified to fix the defect and ensure that the test case of this defect passes successfully.

Continuous integration (CI) is a practice that ensures automating the build and the test process of the application. In continuous integration testing, the tests of the application source code run periodically (for example many times per day) in order to identify the application's potential problems and to reduce the integration time of the application components.

As a result of reducing the regression defects, having good unit testing reduces the test cycle for each phase (or system deployment). In addition to this, the application can have more and more features per iterations or phases peacefully without worrying if these features shall break an existing module that has good unit tests.

What Test-Driven Development (TDD) is

There are two known approaches in writing unit tests for applications.
The first approach prefers writing unit tests after writing the actual application code and this approach is called **traditional unit testing**. The second approach prefers writing unit tests before writing the actual application code, and this approach is called **Test-Driven Development** (TDD) or the **Test-First** approach.

As shown in the following figure, traditional unit testing is about writing the application code first. It can simply be a class or a method. After writing the piece of code, the unit tests, which test the functionality of the code, are written. Then the unit tests run. If the unit tests fail then the developer fixes the defects and runs the unit tests again. If the unit tests succeed then the developer can either refactor the code and run the tests again or continue to write the next piece of code and so on.

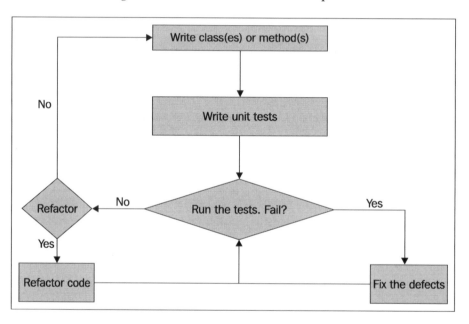

As shown in the following figure, TDD starts by writing a failing unit test to indicate that the functionality is missing. After writing the unit test, the unit test must be run to ensure that it fails. After that, the developer writes the application code that meets the unit test expectation. The unit test must be run again to ensure that it succeeds. If it fails then the developer fixes the bugs and if it succeeds the developer can either refactor the application code or continue writing the next test case.

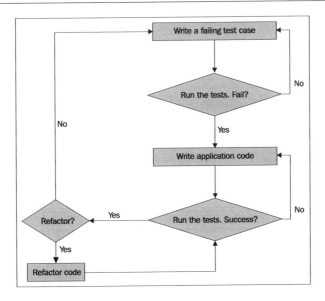

TDD is a powerful technique, as it can give you more control on the application code and design; however, it is a double-edged sword because if it is done incorrectly, writing the tests can waste a lot of time and the schedule of the project can slip. Finally, either you are using TDD or traditional unit testing technique. Don't forget to make your tests automated, repeatable, easy to understand, incremental, easy to run, and fast.

Complexities in testing JavaScript applications

Testing JavaScript applications is complex and requires a lot of time and effort. Testing JavaScript applications requires the tester to test the application on different browsers (Internet Explorer, Firefox, Safari, Chrome, and so on). This is because the JavaScript code that runs on a specific browser will not necessarily work on another browser.

Testing existing JavaScript web applications (with many web pages) on new browsers that are not supported by the application code is not a flexible process. Supporting a new unsupported browser means allocating more time for testing the application again on this new browser and for the new/regression defects to be fixed by the developers. Let's see a simple Broken JavaScript example, which illustrates this idea. In this example, the user enters his/her name and then clicks on the **Welcome** button. After that the welcome message appears.

The following code snippet shows the broken JavaScript example:

```
<!DOCTYPE html>
<html>
<head>
  <title>Broken JavaScript Example</title>
  <script type=»text/javascript»>
    function welcome() {
      var userName = document.getElementById(«userName»).value;
      document.getElementById(«welcomeMessage»).innerText = «Welcome «
      + userName + «!»;
    }
  </script>
</head>
<body>
  <h1>Broken JavaScript Example</h1>

  <label>Please enter your name:</label>
  <input id=»userName» type=»text» /><br/>
  <input type=»button» onclick=»welcome()» value=»Welcome»></
  input><br/><br/>
  <div id=»welcomeMessage»/>

</body>
</html>
```

Downloading the example code

You can download the example code files for all Packt books you have purchased from your account at http://www.PacktPub.com. If you purchased this book elsewhere, you can visit http://www.PacktPub.com/support and register to have the files e-mailed directly to you.

If you run the code shown in the previous code snippet, you will find that it works fine in Internet Explorer (IE) and Safari while it does not work in Firefox (to be more specific, this example works on Internet Explorer 8 and Safari 5.1, while it will not work on Firefox 3.6). The reason behind this problem is that the innerText property is not supported in Firefox. This is one of the hundreds of examples that show a code that works in a specific browser while it does not work in another one.

As a result of these complexities, testing JavaScript code requires a good unit testing tool, which provides mechanisms to overcome these complexities. The *good* JavaScript unit testing tool should be able to execute the test cases across all of the browsers, should have an easy setup, should have an easy configuration, and should be fast in executing the test cases.

Weather forecasting application

Now, let's move to the weather forecasting application. The weather forecasting application is a Java web application that allows the users to check the current weather in different cities in the world. The weather forecasting application contains both synchronous and asynchronous (Ajax) JavaScript code, which we will test in the later chapters of the book using the different JavaScript unit testing frameworks.

The weather forecasting application mainly contains three use cases:

- Log in to the application
- Register a user in the application
- Check the current weather in a specific city

The weather forecasting application is a Java web application. The server-side part of the application is written using Java servlets (`http://docs.oracle.com/javaee/6/tutorial/doc/bnafd.html`). If you are not familiar with Java servlets, do not worry. This book focuses only on JavaScript unit testing; all you need to know about these servlets is the functionality of each one of them, not the code behind it. The functionality of each application servlet will be explained during when the JavaScript code is explained, to show you the complete Ajax request life cycle with the server.

Another thing that needs to be mentioned is that the weather application pages are `.jsp` files; however, 99 percent of their code is pure HTML code that is easy to understand (the application pages code will be explained in detail in the next section).

The first screen of the application is the login screen in which the user enters his username and password, as shown in the following screenshot:

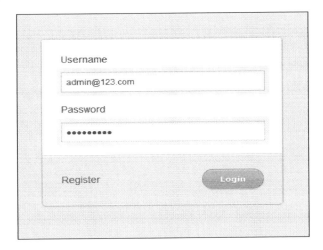

When the user clicks on the **Login** button, there is a JavaScript login client that ensures that the username and the password are entered correctly. If the username and the password are correct, they are submitted to the server, which validates them if the user is registered in the application. If the user is registered in the application then the user is redirected to the weather checking page; otherwise an error message appears to the user.

The username field must not be empty and has to be in a valid e-mail address format. The password field also must not be empty and has to contain at least one digit, one capital, one small character, and at least one special character. The password length has to be six characters or more.

In the weather checking page, the user can select one of the available cities from the combobox, then click on the **Get weather condition** button to get the current weather information of the selected city, as shown in the following screenshot:

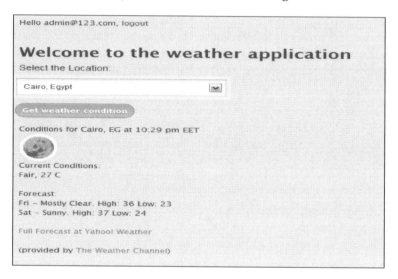

In the user registration page, the user can register in the application by entering his username and confirmed password, as shown in the following screenshot:

When the user clicks on the **Register** button, the registration client's JavaScript object ensures that the username and the passwords are entered correctly. The registration client uses the same rules of the login client in username and password validations. It also ensures that the confirmed password is the same as the entered password.

If the user's registration information is correct, the username and passwords are submitted to the server. The user information is registered in the system after performing server-side validations and checking that the user has not already registered in the application. If the user is already registered in the system then an error message appears to the user.

Exploring the application's HTML and JavaScript code

The following code snippet shows the HTML code of the login form in the `login.jsp` file. It is a simple form that has username and password fields with their labels, messages, a registration link, and a login button.

```
<form class="box login" action="/weatherApplication/LoginServlet"
method="post">
  <fieldset class="boxBody">
    <label for="username">Username  <span id="usernameMessage"
     class="error"></span></label>
    <input type="text" id="username" name="username"/>

    <label for="password">Password  <span id="passwordMessage"
     class="error"></span></label>
    <input type="password" id="password" name="password"/>
  </fieldset>
  <div id="footer">
```

```
   <label><a href="register.jsp">Register</a></label>
   <input id="btnLogin" class="btnLogin" type="submit" value="Login"
    onclick="return validateLoginForm();"/>
 </div>
</form>
```

When the **Login** button is clicked, the `validateLoginForm` JavaScript function is called. The following code snippet shows the `validateLoginForm` function in the `login.jsp` file:

```
function validateLoginForm() {
  var loginClient = new weatherapp.LoginClient();

  var loginForm = {
    "userNameField" : "username",
    "passwordField" : "password",
    "userNameMessage" : "usernameMessage",
    "passwordMessage" : "passwordMessage"
  };

  return loginClient.validateLoginForm(loginForm);
}
```

The `validateLoginForm` function calls the `LoginClient` JavaScript object that is responsible for validating the login form. It constructs a **JavaScript Object Notation (JSON)** object that includes the username, password, username message, and password message IDs, and then passes the constructed JSON object to the `validateLoginForm` function of the `LoginClient` object.

 The weather application customizes a CSS3 based style from the blog CSS Junction:

http://www.cssjunction.com/freebies/simple-login-from-html5css3-template-free/

The following code snippet shows the `validateLoginForm` method of the `LoginClient` object in the `LoginClient.js` file. It validates that the username and the password fields are not empty and are compliant with the validation rules.

```
if (typeof weatherapp == "undefined" || !weatherapp) {
  weatherapp = {};
}

weatherapp.LoginClient = function() {};

weatherapp.LoginClient.prototype.validateLoginForm =
```

```
function(loginForm) {

  if (this.validateEmptyFields(loginForm) &&
      this.validateUserName(loginForm) &&
        this.validatePassword(loginForm)) {

    return true;
  }

  return false;
};
```

One of the recommended JavaScript's best practices is to use namespaces; the application defines a JavaScript namespace in order to avoid collisions with other JavaScript objects of similar names. The following code defines a `weatherapp` namespace if it is not already defined:

```
if (typeof weatherapp == "undefined" || !weatherapp) {
  weatherapp = {};
}
```

The following code snippet shows the `validateEmptyFields` method of the `LoginClient` object in the `LoginClient.js` file. It validates that the username and the password fields are not empty and if any of these fields are empty, an error message appears:

```
weatherapp.LoginClient.prototype.validateEmptyFields =
function(loginForm) {
  var passwordMessageID = loginForm.passwordMessage;
  var userNameMessageID = loginForm.userNameMessage;

  var passwordFieldID = loginForm.passwordField;
  var userNameFieldID = loginForm.userNameField;

  document.getElementById(passwordMessageID).innerHTML = "";
  document.getElementById(userNameMessageID).innerHTML = "";

  if (! document.getElementById(userNameFieldID).value) {
    document.getElementById(userNameMessageID).innerHTML = "(field is
    required)";

    return false;
  }
```

```
if (! document.getElementById(passwordFieldID).value) {
   document.getElementById(passwordMessageID).innerHTML = "(field is
   required)";

   return false;
}

   return true;
};
```

The following code snippet shows the `validateUserName` method of the
`LoginClient` object in the `LoginClient.js` file. It validates that the username
is in the form of a valid e-mail:

```
weatherapp.LoginClient.prototype.validateUserName =
function(loginForm) {

   // the username must be an email...
   var userNameMessageID = loginForm.userNameMessage;
   var userNameFieldID = loginForm.userNameField;

   var userNameRegex = /^[_A-Za-z0-9-]+(\.[_A-Za-z0-9-]+)*@
[A-Za-z0-9]+(\.[A-Za-z0-9]+)*(\.[A-Za-z]{2,})$/;
   var userName = document.getElementById(userNameFieldID).value;

   if(! userNameRegex.test(userName)) {
      document.getElementById(userNameMessageID).innerHTML = "(format is
      invalid)";

   return false;
}

      return true;
};
```

Using the regular expression `/^[_A-Za-z0-9-]+(\.[_A-Za-z0-9-]+)*@
[A-Za-z0-9]+(\.[A-Za-z0-9]+)*(\.[A-Za-z]{2,})$/`, the username is validated
against a valid e-mail form. If the username is not in a valid e-mail form then an
error message appears in the username message span.

The following code snippet shows the `validatePassword` method of the
`LoginClient` object in the `LoginClient.js` file. It validates if the password has
at least one digit, one capital character, one small character, at least one special
character, and also if it contains six characters or more:

```
weatherapp.LoginClient.prototype.validatePassword =
```

```
function(loginForm) {

    // the password contains at least one digit, one capital and small
character
    // and at least one special character, and 6 characters or more...
    var passwordMessageID = loginForm.passwordMessage;
    var passwordFieldID = loginForm.passwordField;

    var passwordRegex = /((?=.*\d)(?=.*[a-z])(?=.*[A-Z])(?=.*[@#$%]).
{6,20})/;
    var password = document.getElementById(passwordFieldID).value;

    if (! (passwordRegex.test(password) && password.length >= 6)) {
        document.getElementById(passwordMessageID).innerHTML = "(format is
        invalid)";

        return false;
    }

    return true;
};
```

If the password is not compliant with the mentioned rules then an error message appears in the password message span.

If the username and the password fields pass the JavaScript validation rules, the login form submits its content to LoginServlet, which makes another server-side validation and then redirects the user to the weather checking page if the validation goes OK.

 It is very important not to rely on the JavaScript client-side validation only, because JavaScript can be disabled from the browser. So it is a must to always make a server-side validation besides the client-side validation.

The following code snippet shows the weather checking form of the weather application located in the welcome.jsp file. It contains a combobox filled with the Yahoo! Weather Where On Earth IDs (the WOEID is a unique reference identifier assigned by Yahoo! to identify any place on Earth) of different cities in the world.

```
<h1>Welcome to the weather application</h1>
<FORM method="post">
    <label class="label" for="postalCode">Select the Location: </label>
    <select id="w" class="selectField">
        <option value="1521894">Cairo, Egypt</option>
```

```
        <option value="906057">Stockholm, Sweden</option>
        <option value="551801">Vienna, Austria</option>
        <option value="766273">Madrid, Spain</option>
        <option value="615702">Paris, France</option>
        <option value="2459115">New York, USA</option>
        <option value="418440">Lima, Peru</option>
    </select>

    <input type="button" class="button" onclick="invokeWeatherClient();"
           value="Get weather condition"/>
    <br/><br/>

    <div id="weatherInformation" class="weatherPanel">
    </div>
</FORM>
```

When the **Get weather condition** button is clicked, the invokeWeatherClient function is called. The following code snippet shows the invokeWeatherClient function code in the welcome.jsp file:

```
function invokeWeatherClient() {
  var weatherClient = new weatherapp.WeatherClient();
  var location = document.getElementById("w").value;

  weatherClient.getWeatherCondition({
    'location': location,
    'resultDivID': 'weatherInformation'
  },
weatherClient.displayWeatherInformation,
weatherClient.handleWeatherInfoError);
}
```

The invokeWeatherClient function calls the getWeatherCondition method of the WeatherClient object. The first parameter of the getWeatherCondition method is the weatherForm object, which is a JSON object containing the location WOEID and the ID of the DIV element that receives the weather information HTML result of the Yahoo! Weather Representational State Transfer (REST) service. The second parameter represents the first callback, which is the displayWeatherInformation method that is called if the getWeatherCondition call succeeds. The last parameter represents the second callback, which is the handleWeatherInfoError method that is called if the getWeatherCondition call fails.

The following code snippet shows getWeatherCondition of the WeatherClient object in the WeatherClient.js file that sends an Ajax request to WeatherProxyServlet with the w parameter that represents the **WOEID**.

`WeatherProxyServlet` interacts with the Yahoo! Weather REST service in order to fetch the current weather information:

```
if (typeof weatherapp == "undefined" || !weatherapp) {
  weatherapp = {};
}

weatherapp.WeatherClient = function() {};
weatherapp.WeatherClient.xmlhttp;
weatherapp.WeatherClient.weatherForm;
weatherapp.WeatherClient.endpointURL = "";

weatherapp.WeatherClient.prototype.getWeatherCondition =
function(weatherForm, successCallBack, failureCallBack) {

  if (window.XMLHttpRequest) {
    this.xmlhttp = new XMLHttpRequest();
  } else {
    this.xmlhttp = new ActiveXObject("Microsoft.XMLHTTP");
  }

  var successCallBackLocal = successCallBack;
  var failureCallBackLocal = failureCallBack;
  var weatherClientLocal = this;

  this.xmlhttp.onreadystatechange = function() {
weatherClientLocal.weatherInformationReady(successCallBackLocal,
failureCallBackLocal);
  };

  this.weatherForm = weatherForm;

  if (typeof this.endpointURL == "undefined") {
    this.endpointURL = "";
  }

  this.xmlhttp.open("GET",
        this.endpointURL +
        "/weatherApplication/WeatherProxyServlet?w=" + weatherForm.
          location + "&preventCache=" + new Date().getTime(),
        true);

  this.xmlhttp.send();
};
```

```
weatherapp.WeatherClient.prototype.weatherInformationReady =
function(successCallBack, failureCallBack) {
  if (this.xmlhttp.readyState != 4) {
    return;
  }

  if (this.xmlhttp.status != 200)  {
    failureCallBack(this);

return;
      }

  if (this.xmlhttp.readyState == 4 && this.xmlhttp.status == 200) {
    successCallBack(this);
      }
};

weatherapp.WeatherClient.prototype.displayWeatherInformation =
function(weatherClient) {
  var resultDivID = weatherClient.weatherForm.resultDivID;

document.getElementById(resultDivID).innerHTML = weatherClient.
xmlhttp.responseText;
};

weatherapp.WeatherClient.prototype.handleWeatherInfoError =
function(weatherClient) {
  var resultDivID = weatherClient.weatherForm.resultDivID;

  alert ("Error: " + weatherClient.xmlhttp.responseText);
document.getElementById(resultDivID).innerHTML = "Error: " +
weatherClient.xmlhttp.responseText;
};
```

The getWeatherCondition method first creates an XML HTTP request object using new XMLHttpRequest() in case of IE7+, Firefox, Chrome, and Opera. In the case of IE5 and IE6, the XML HTTP request object is created using an ActiveX object new ActiveXObject("Microsoft.XMLHTTP").

The getWeatherCondition method then registers both, the success callback (successCallBack) and the failure callback (failureCallBack) using the weatherInformationReady method that is called for every Ajax readyState change.

Finally, the `getWeatherCondition` method sends an asynchronous Ajax request to `WeatherProxyServlet`. When the Ajax response comes from the server and the operation is done successfully then the success callback is called, which is the `displayWeatherInformation` method. In the case of operation failure (which can happen, for example, if the passed WOEID is invalid or the Yahoo! Weather service is down), the failure callback is called, which is the `handleWeatherInfoError` method.

The `displayWeatherInformation` method displays the returned weather information HTML result from `WeatherProxyServlet` (which fetches the weather information from the Yahoo! Weather REST service) in the `weatherInformation` div element while the `handleWeatherInfoError` method displays the error message in the same div element and also displays an alert with the error message.

It is assumed that you are familiar with Ajax programming. If you are not familiar with Ajax programming, it is recommended to check the following introductory Ajax tutorial on w3schools:

`http://www.w3schools.com/ajax/default.asp`

In order to prevent IE from caching Ajax GET requests, a random parameter is appended using `new Date().getTime()`. In many JavaScript libraries, this can be handled through the framework APIs. For example, in Dojo the `preventCache` attribute of the `dojo.xhrGet` API can be used to prevent the IE Ajax GET caching.

The following code snippet shows the HTML code of the registration form in the `register.jsp` file. It consists of a username and two password fields with their corresponding labels, messages, login link, and a register button:

```
<form class="box register" method="post">
  <fieldset class="boxBody">

<label for="username">Username (Email)  <span id="usernameMessage"
class="error"></span></label>
    <input type="text" id="username" name="username"/>

<label for="password1">Password  <span id="passwordMessage1"
class="error"></span></label>
    <input type="password" id="password1" name="password1"/>

    <label for="password2">Confirm your password</label>
    <input type="password" id="password2" name="password2"/>

  </fieldset>
  <div id="footer">
    <label><a href="login.jsp">Login</a></label>
```

```
<input id="btnRegister" class="btnLogin" type="button"
value="Register" onclick="registerUser();" />
    </div>

</form>
```

When the **Register** button is clicked, the `registerUser` JavaScript function is called. The following code snippet shows the code of the `registerUser` function in the `register.jsp` file:

```
function registerUser() {
  var registrationClient = new weatherapp.RegistrationClient();

  var registrationForm = {
    "userNameField" : "username",
    "passwordField1" : "password1",
    "passwordField2" : "password2",
    "userNameMessage" : "usernameMessage",
    "passwordMessage1" : "passwordMessage1"
  };

  if (registrationClient.validateRegistrationForm(registrationForm)) {

    registrationClient.registerUser(registrationForm,
                    registrationClient.displaySuccessMessage,
                        registrationClient.handleRegistrationError);
  }
}
```

The `registerUser` function is calling the `RegistrationClient` JavaScript object that is responsible for validating and submitting the registration form using Ajax to `RegistrationServlet`. `registerUser` constructs the `registrationForm` JSON object, which includes the username, password1, password2, username message, and password1 message IDs, and then passes the object to the `validateRegistrationForm` method of the `RegistrationClient` object.

If the validation passes, it calls the `registerUser` method of the `RegistrationClient` object. The first parameter of the `registerUser` method is the `registrationForm` JSON object. The second parameter is the success callback, which is the `displaySuccessMessage` method, while the last parameter is the failure callback, which is the `handleRegistrationError` method.

The following code snippet shows the code of the `validateRegistrationForm` method of the `RegistrationClient` object in the `RegistrationClient.js` file. It uses the validation methods of `LoginClient` in order to validate the empty username and password fields, and to validate if the username and the password fields conform to the validation rules. In addition to this, the `validateRegistrationForm` method validates if the two entered passwords are identical:

```
if (typeof weatherapp == "undefined" || !weatherapp) {
  weatherapp = {};
}

weatherapp.RegistrationClient = function() {};
weatherapp.RegistrationClient.xmlhttp;
weatherapp.RegistrationClient.endpointURL = "";

weatherapp.RegistrationClient.prototype.validateRegistrationForm =
function(registrationForm) {
  var userNameMessage = registrationForm.userNameMessage;
  var passwordMessage1 = registrationForm.passwordMessage1;

  var userNameField = registrationForm.userNameField;
  var passwordField1 = registrationForm.passwordField1;
  var passwordField2 = registrationForm.passwordField2;

  var password1 = document.getElementById(passwordField1).value;
  var password2 = document.getElementById(passwordField2).value;

  // Empty messages ...
  document.getElementById(userNameMessage).innerHTML = "";
  document.getElementById(passwordMessage1).innerHTML = "";

  // create the loginClient object in order to validate fields ...
  var loginClient = new weatherapp.LoginClient();

  var loginForm = {};

  loginForm.userNameField = userNameField;
  loginForm.userNameMessage = userNameMessage;
  loginForm.passwordField = passwordField1;
  loginForm.passwordMessage = passwordMessage1;

  // validate empty username and password fields.
  if (! loginClient.validateEmptyFields(loginForm)) {
    return false;
  }

  // validate that password fields have the same value...
```

```
    if (password1 != password2) {
document.getElementById(passwordMessage1).innerHTML = "(Passwords must
be identical)";

    return false;
}

    // check if the username is correct...
    if (! loginClient.validateUserName(loginForm) ) {
document.getElementById(userNameMessage).innerHTML = "(format is
invalid)";

    return false;
}

    // check if the password is correct...
    if (! loginClient.validatePassword(loginForm) ) {
document.getElementById(passwordMessage1).innerHTML = "(format is
invalid)";

    return false;
}

    return true;
};
```

The following code snippet shows the `registerUser` method code of the `RegistrationClient` object in the `RegistrationClient.js` file. It creates an Ajax POST request with the username and the passwords' (original password and confirmed password) data and sends them asynchronously to `RegistrationServlet`.

```
weatherapp.RegistrationClient.prototype.registerUser =
function(registrationForm, successCallBack, failureCallBack) {
    var userNameField = registrationForm.userNameField;
    var passwordField1 = registrationForm.passwordField1;
    var passwordField2 = registrationForm.passwordField2;

    var userName = document.getElementById(userNameField).value;
    var password1 = document.getElementById(passwordField1).value;
    var password2 = document.getElementById(passwordField2).value;

    if (window.XMLHttpRequest) {
      this.xmlhttp = new XMLHttpRequest();
    } else {
      this.xmlhttp = new ActiveXObject("Microsoft.XMLHTTP");
    }
```

```
  var successCallBackLocal = successCallBack;
  var failureCallBackLocal = failureCallBack;
  var registrationClientLocal = this;

  this.xmlhttp.onreadystatechange = function() {
registrationClientLocal.registrationReady(successCallBackLocal,
failureCallBackLocal);
  };

  if (typeof this.endpointURL == "undefined") {
    this.endpointURL = "";
  }

  this.xmlhttp.open("POST",
          this.endpointURL +
          "/weatherApplication/RegistrationServlet",
           true);

this.xmlhttp.setRequestHeader("Content-type","application/x-www-form-
urlencoded");

  this.xmlhttp.send(userNameField + "=" + userName + "&" +
          passwordField1 + "=" + password1 + "&" +
          passwordField2 + "=" + password2);
};

weatherapp.RegistrationClient.prototype.registrationReady =
function(successCallBack, failureCallBack) {
  if (this.xmlhttp.readyState != 4) {
    return;
  }

  if (this.xmlhttp.status != 200)  {
    failureCallBack(this);
return;
}

  if (this.xmlhttp.readyState == 4 && this.xmlhttp.status == 200) {
    successCallBack(this);
      }
};

weatherapp.RegistrationClient.prototype.displaySuccessMessage =
function(registrationClient) {
  alert("User registration went successfully ...");
};


weatherapp.RegistrationClient.prototype.handleRegistrationError =
```

```
function(registrationClient) {
  alert(registrationClient.xmlhttp.responseText);
};
```

`RegistrationServlet` validates the user data and ensures that the user did not already register in the application. When the Ajax response comes from the server, and the registration operation is completed successfully, the `displaySuccessMessage` method is called. If the registration operation failed (for example, if the user ID is already registered in the application), the `handleRegistrationError` method is called. Both the `displaySuccessMessage` and the `handleRegistrationError` methods display alerts to show the success and the failure registration messages.

Running the weather application

In order to run the weather application, you first need to download the `weatherApplication.war` file from the book's website (`www.packtpub.com`). Then you need to deploy the WAR file on Apache Tomcat 6. In order to install Apache Tomcat 6, you need to download it from `http://tomcat.apache.org/download-60.cgi`. Apache Tomcat 6.0 requires the Java 2 Standard Edition Runtime Environment (JRE) Version 5.0 or later.

In order to install JRE, you need to download and install the J2SE Runtime Environment as follows:

1. Download the JRE, release Version 5.0 or later, from `http://www.oracle.com/technetwork/java/javase/downloads/index.html`.
2. Install the JRE according to the instructions included with the release.
3. Set an environment variable named `JRE_HOME` to the pathname of the directory in which you installed the JRE, for example, `c:\jre5.0` or `/usr/local/java/jre5.0`.

After you download the binary distribution of Apache Tomcat 6, you need to unpack the distribution in a suitable location on the hard disk. After this, you need to define the `CATALINA_HOME` environment variable, which refers to the location of the Tomcat distribution.

Now, you can start Apache Tomcat 6 by executing the following command on Windows:

```
$CATALINA_HOME\bin\startup.bat
```

Start as while in Unix, you can execute the following command:

`$CATALINA_HOME/bin/startup.sh`

In order to make sure that the Apache Tomcat 6 starts correctly, you need to type the following URL in the browser:

`http://localhost:8080/`

After making sure that the Apache Tomcat 6 is running correctly, you can stop it by executing the following command on Windows:

`$CATALINA_HOME\bin\shutdown.bat`

Start as while in Unix, you can execute the following command:

`$CATALINA_HOME/bin/shutdown.sh`

Now, we come to the step of the weather application deployment where you need to get the `weatherApplication.war` file from the book resources. After getting the file, copy the WAR file to the `$CATALINA_HOME\webapps` folder, then start the Apache Tomcat 6 again.

In order to access the weather application, you can access it using the following URL:

`http://localhost:8080/weatherApplication/login.jsp`

 For the sake of simplicity, there is a predefined username and password that can be used to access the weather application; the username is `admin@123.com` and the password is `Admin@123`. Another thing that has to be mentioned is that the registered users are not stored in a database; they are stored in the application scope, which means they will be available as long as the application is not restarted.

Summary

In this chapter, you learned what unit testing is, the requirements of a good unit test, and why we need unit testing. You got to know the difference between the Test-Driven Development and the traditional unit testing. In the JavaScript world, you understood the complexities of testing JavaScript code, and the requirements of good JavaScript unit testing tools. At the end of this chapter, I explored with you the weather web application use cases and its JavaScript code in detail, which we will unit test in the later chapters. In the next chapter, you will learn how to work with the Jasmine framework and how to use it for testing the weather application.

2
Jasmine

Jasmine is a powerful JavaScript unit testing framework. It provides a clean mechanism for testing synchronous and asynchronous JavaScript code. Jasmine is a behavior-driven development framework that provides descriptive test cases that focus more on the business value than on the technical details. Because it is written in a simple natural language, Jasmine tests can be read by non-programmers and can provide a clear description when a single test succeeds or fails and also the reason behind its failure. In this chapter, the framework will be illustrated in detail and will be used to test the weather application that is discussed in *Chapter 1, Unit Testing JavaScript Applications*.

Behavior-driven development (BDD) is an agile software development technique introduced by Dan North that focuses on writing descriptive tests from the business perspective. BDD extends TDD by writing test cases that test the software behavior (requirements) in a natural language that anyone (not necessarily a programmer) can read and understand. The names of the unit tests are sentences that usually start with the word "should" and they are written in the order of their business value.

Configuration

In order to configure Jasmine, the first step is to download the framework from `https://github.com/pivotal/jasmine/downloads`. Here, you will find the latest releases of the framework. At the time of this writing, the latest release is v1.2.0, which has been used in this book.

After unpacking `jasmine-standalone-1.2.0.zip` (or later), you will find the folder structure shown in the following screenshot:

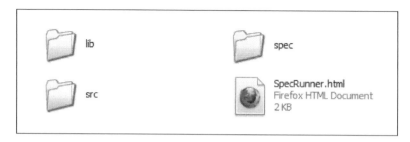

The `src` folder in the preceding screenshot contains the JavaScript source files that you want to test, the `spec` folder contains the JavaScript testing files, while `SpecRunner.html` is the test case runner HTML file. The `lib` folder contains the framework files.

In order to make sure that everything is running OK, click on the `SpecRunner.html` file; you should see passing specs, as shown in the following screenshot:

```
Jasmine 1.2.0 revision 1337005947

• • • • •

Passing 5 specs

Player
   should be able to play a Song

   when song has been paused
      should indicate that the song is currently paused
      should be possible to resume
   tells the current song if the user has made it a favorite

   #resume
      should throw an exception if song is already playing
```

This structure is not rigid; you can modify it to serve the organization of your application. For the purpose of testing the weather application, we will modify it to cope with the structure of the application.

Writing your first Jasmine test

Before writing the first Jasmine test, we will need to understand the difference between a suite and a spec (test specification) in Jasmine. A Jasmine **suite** is a group of test cases that can be used to test a specific behavior of the JavaScript code (a JavaScript object or function). In Jasmine, the test suite begins with a call to the Jasmine global function `describe` with two parameters. The first parameter represents the title of the test suite, while the second parameter represents a function that implements the test suite.

A Jasmine **spec** represents a test case inside the test suite. In Jasmine, a test case begins with a call to the Jasmine global function `it` with two parameters. The first parameter represents the title of the spec and the second parameter represents a function that implements the test case.

A Jasmine spec contains one or more expectations. Every expectation represents an assertion that can be either `true` or `false`. In order to pass the spec, all of the expectations inside the spec have to be true. If one or more expectations inside a spec is false, the spec fails. The following code snippet shows an example of a Jasmine test suite and a spec with an expectation:

```
describe("A sample suite", function() {
  it("contains a sample spec with an expectation", function() {
    expect(true).toEqual(true);
  });
});
```

Now, let's move to the `SimpleMath` JavaScript object, which is described in the following code snippet. The `SimpleMath` JavaScript object is a simple mathematical utility that performs factorial, signum, and average mathematical operations.

```
SimpleMath = function() {
};

SimpleMath.prototype.getFactorial = function (number) {

  if (number < 0) {
    throw new Error("There is no factorial for negative numbers");
  }
  else if (number == 1 || number == 0) {

    // If number <= 1 then number! = 1.
      return 1;
  } else {

    // If number > 1 then number! = number * (number-1)!
      return number * this.getFactorial(number-1);
  }
}
```

```
SimpleMath.prototype.signum = function (number) {
    if (number > 0)  {
    return 1;
    } else if (number == 0) {
    return 0;
    } else {
    return -1;
    }
}


SimpleMath.prototype.average = function (number1, number2) {
    return (number1 + number2) / 2;
}
```

In the preceding code snippet, the `SimpleMath` object is used to calculate the factorial of numbers. In mathematics, the factorial function of a nonnegative integer *n*, which is denoted by *n!*, is the product of all positive integers less than or equal to *n*. For example, *4! = 4 x 3 x 2 x 1 = 24*. According to Wikipedia, the factorial function has the following mathematical definition:

$$n! = \begin{cases} 1 & \text{if } n = 0, \\ (n-1)! \times n & \text{if } n > 0. \end{cases}$$

The `SimpleMath` object calculates the factorial of the number using the `getFactorial` recursive function. It throws an `Error` exception when the passed parameter to the `getFactorial` method is a negative number because there is no factorial value for negative numbers.

In addition to calculating the factorial of numbers, it can get the signum of any number using the `signum` method. In mathematics, the signum function extracts the sign of a real number. According to Wikipedia, the signum function has the following mathematical definition:

$$\text{sgn}(x) = \begin{cases} -1 & \text{if } x < 0, \\ 0 & \text{if } x = 0, \\ 1 & \text{if } x > 0. \end{cases}$$

Finally, `SimpleMath` can calculate the average of two numbers using the `average` method. The average value of two numbers can be calculated by dividing the sum of the two numbers by 2.

Now, let's start writing the specs using Jasmine. First of all, in order to test the `getFactorial` method, let's have the three following test scenarios; we will test calculating the factorial of:

- A positive number
- Zero
- A negative number

 Boundary testing is a kind of testing that focuses on the boundary or the limit conditions of the objects to be tested. These boundary conditions can include the maximum value, minimum value, error values, and inside/outside boundary values. In the factorial testing example, the test scenarios apply this kind of testing by testing the factorial API with a positive number, a negative number, and zero.

The following code snippet shows how to test the calculation of the factorial of a positive number (3), 0, and a negative number (-10):

```
describe("SimpleMath", function() {
  var simpleMath;

  beforeEach(function() {
      simpleMath = new SimpleMath();
  });

  describe("when SimpleMath is used to find factorial", function() {
      it("should be able to find factorial for positive number",
         function() {
      expect(simpleMath.getFactorial(3)).toEqual(6);
      });

      it("should be able to find factorial for zero", function() {
      expect(simpleMath.getFactorial(0)).toEqual(1);
      });

      it("should be able to throw an exception when the number is
         negative", function() {
      expect(
        function() {
          simpleMath.getFactorial(-10)
        }).toThrow("There is no factorial for negative numbers");
      });

  });
  ...
});
```

The `describe` keyword declares a new test suite called `"SimpleMath"`. `beforeEach` is used for initialization of the specs inside the suite, that is, `beforeEach` is called once before the run of each spec in the `describe` function. In the `beforeEach` function, the `simpleMath` object is created using `new SimpleMath()`.

> In Jasmine, it is also possible to execute JavaScript code after the run of each spec in the `describe` function, using the `afterEach` global function. Having `beforeEach` and `afterEach` in Jasmine allows the developer not to repeat setup and finalization code for each spec.

After initializing the `simpleMath` object, you can either create a direct spec using the `it` keyword or create a child test suite using the `describe` keyword. For the purpose of organizing the example, a new test suite is created for each group of tests with similar functionalities. This is why an independent test suite is created to test the functionality of the `getFactorial` test suite provided by the `SimpleMath` object using the `describe` keyword.

In the first test scenario of the `getFactorial` test suite, the spec title is `"should be able to find factorial for positive number"`, and the `expect` function calls `simpleMath.getFactorial(3)` and expects it to be equal to 6. If `simpleMath.getFactorial(3)` returns a value other than 6, the test fails. We have many other options (matchers) to use instead of `toEqual`. These matchers will be discussed in more detail in the *Jasmine matchers* section.

In the second test scenario of the `getFactorial` test suite, the `expect` function calls `simpleMath.getFactorial(0)` and expects it to be equal to 1. In the last test scenario of the `getFactorial` test suite, the `expect` function calls `simpleMath.getFactorial(-10)` and expects it to throw an exception with the message `"There is no factorial for negative numbers"`, using the `toThrow` matcher. The `toThrow` matcher succeeds if the function `expect` throws an exception when executed.

After finalizing the `getFactorial` test suite, we come to a new test suite that tests the functionality of the `signum` method provided by the `SimpleMath` object. The following code snippet shows the signum test suite:

```
describe("when SimpleMath is used to find signum", function() {
    it("should be able to find the signum for a positive number",
      function() {
      expect(simpleMath.signum(3)).toEqual(1);
    });

    it("should be able to find the signum for zero", function() {
      expect(simpleMath.signum(0)).toEqual(0);
    });
```

```
it("should be able to find the signum for a negative number",
    function() {
  expect(simpleMath.signum(-1000)).toEqual(-1);
});
});
```

We have three test scenarios for the `signum` method, the first test scenario is about getting the signum value for a positive number, the second test scenario is about getting the signum value for zero, and the last test scenario is about getting the signum value for a negative number. As indicated in the definition of the signum function, it has to return +1 for any positive number, 0 for zero, and finally -1 for any negative number. The following code snippet shows the average test suite:

```
describe("when SimpleMath is used to find the average of two
            values", function() {
    it("should be able to find the average of two values",
        function() {
    expect(simpleMath.average(3, 6)).toEqual(4.5);
      });
});
```

In the `average` spec, the test ensures that the average is calculated correctly by trying to calculate the average of two numbers, 3 and 6, and expecting the result to be 4.5.

Now, after writing the suites and the specs, it is the time to run the tests. In order to run the tests, we need to do the following steps:

1. Place the `simpleMath.js` file in the `src` folder.

2. Place the `simpleMathSpec.js` file, which contains the `SimpleMath` unit tests, in the `spec` folder.

3. Edit the `SpecRunner.html` file as shown in the following code snippet:

```
<html>
<head>
  <title>Jasmine Spec Runner</title>

  <link rel="shortcut icon" type="image/png"
  href="lib/jasmine-1.2.0/jasmine_favicon.png">
  <link rel="stylesheet" type="text/css" href="lib/jasmine-
  1.2.0/jasmine.css">
  <script type="text/javascript" src="lib/jasmine-
  1.2.0/jasmine.js"></script>
  <script type="text/javascript" src="lib/jasmine-
  1.2.0/jasmine-html.js"></script>
```

```
<!-- include spec files here... -->
<script type="text/javascript"
src="spec/simpleMathSpec.js"></script>

<!-- include source files here... -->
<script type="text/javascript"
src="src/simpleMath.js"></script>
```

As shown in the preceding code snippet, in the highlighted lines, `<script type="text/javascript" src="spec/simpleMathSpec.js"></script>` is added under the `<!-- include spec files here... -->` section, while `<script type="text/javascript" src="src/simpleMath.js"></script>` is added under the `<!-- include source files here... -->` section. After double-clicking on `SpecRunner.html`, you will see the test results passed.

The nested describe blocks

Jasmine is flexible in nesting the `describe` blocks with specs at any level. This means that, before executing a spec, Jasmine walks down executing each `beforeEach` function in order, then executes the spec, and lastly walks up executing each `afterEach` function.

The following code snippet is an example of the Jasmine's nested `describe` blocks:

```
describe("MyTest", function() {
  beforeEach(function() {
  alert("beforeEach level1");
  });
  describe("MyTest level2", function() {
          beforeEach(function() {
    alert("beforeEach level2");
    });
    describe("MyTest level3", function() {
      beforeEach(function() {
      alert("beforeEach level3");
      });
      it("is a simple spec in level3", function() {
      alert("A simple spec in level3");
      expect(true).toBe(true);
      });
      afterEach(function() {
      alert("afterEach level3");
      });
    });
```

```
        afterEach(function() {
        alert("afterEach level2");
        });
      });
      afterEach(function() {
      alert("afterEach level1");
      });

});
```

This test will result in the following messages on the alert boxes:

- **beforeEach level1**
- **beforeEach level2**
- **beforeEach level3**
- **A simple spec in level3**
- **afterEach level3**
- **afterEach level2**
- **afterEach level1**

Jasmine matchers

In the first Jasmine example, we used the `toEqual` and `toThrow` Jasmine matchers. In this section, the other different built-in matchers provided by Jasmine will be illustrated and will explain how to write a custom Jasmine matcher to have more powerful and descriptive testing code.

The toBe matcher

The `toBe` matcher is passed if the actual value is of the same type and value as that of the expected value. It uses `===` to perform this comparison. The following code snippet shows an example of the `toBe` matcher:

```
describe("the toBe Matcher", function() {
    it("should compare both types and values", function() {
      var actual = "123";
      var expected = "123";

      expect(actual).toBe(expected);
    });
});
```

You might question the difference between the `toBe` and `toEqual` matchers. The answer to this question would be that the `toEqual` matcher provides a powerful mechanism for handling equality; it can handle array comparisons, for example, as shown in the following code snippet:

```
describe("the toEqual Matcher", function() {
    it("should be able to compare arrays", function() {
      var actual = [1, 2, 3];
      var expected = [1, 2, 3];

      expect(actual).toEqual(expected);
    });
});
```

The following code snippet shows how the `toBe` matcher is unable to compare two equivalent arrays:

```
describe("the toBe Matcher", function() {
    it("should not be able to compare arrays", function() {
      var actual = [1, 2, 3];
        var expected = [1, 2, 3];

      expect(actual).not.toBe(expected);
    });

});
```

As you may have noticed in the preceding code snippet, the `not` keyword is used for making the test passes because the `toBe` matcher will not be able to know that the `actual` and `expected` arrays are the same. The Jasmine `not` keyword can be used with every matcher's criteria for inverting the result.

The toBeDefined and toBeUndefined matchers

The `toBeDefined` matcher is used to ensure that a property or a value is defined, while the `toBeUndefined` matcher is used to ensure that a property or a value is undefined. The following code snippet shows an example of both matchers:

```
describe("the toBeDefined Matcher", function() {
    it("should be able to check defined objects", function() {
      var object = [1, 2, 3];

      expect(object).toBeDefined();
```

```
    });
  });

  describe("the toBeUndefined Matcher", function() {
    it("should be able to check undefined objects", function() {
      var object;

      expect(object).toBeUndefined();
    });
  });
```

You can achieve the behavior of the `toBeUndefined` matcher by using the `not` keyword and the `toBeDefined` matcher, as shown in the following code snippet:

```
  describe("the toBeUndefined Matcher using the not keyword and the
  toBeDefined matcher", function() {
    it("should be able to check undefined objects", function() {
      var object;
      expect(object).not.toBeDefined();
    });
  });
```

The toBeNull matcher

The `toBeNull` matcher is used to ensure that a property or a value is null. The following code snippet shows an example of the `toBeNull` matcher:

```
    describe("the toBeNull Matcher", function() {
      it("should be able to check if an object value is null",
      function() {
        var object = null;

        expect(object).toBeNull();
      });
    });
```

The toBeTruthy and toBeFalsy matchers

The `toBeTruthy` matcher is used to ensure that a property or a value is `true` while the `toBeFalsy` matcher is used for ensuring that a property or a value is `false`. The following code snippet shows an example of both matchers:

```
  describe("the toBeTruthy Matcher", function() {
      it("should be able to check if an object value is true",
  function() {
```

```
        var object = true;
        expect(object).toBeTruthy();
    });
});

describe("the toBeFalsy Matcher", function() {
    it("should be able to check if an object value is false",
function() {
        var object = false;

        expect(object).toBeFalsy();
    });
});
```

The toContain matcher

The toContain matcher is used to check whether a string or array contains a substring or an item. The following code snippet shows an example of the toContain matcher:

```
describe("the toContain Matcher", function() {
    it("should be able to check if a String contains a specific
    substring", function() {
      expect("Hello World from Cairo").toContain("Cairo");
    });

    it("should be able to check if an Array contains a specific
    item", function() {
      expect(["TV", "Watch", "Table"]).toContain("Watch");
    });
});
```

The toBeLessThan and toBeGreaterThan matchers

The toBeLessThan and the toBeGreaterThan matchers are used to perform the simple mathematical less-than and greater-than operations, as shown in the following code snippet:

```
describe("the toBeLessThan Matcher", function() {
    it("should be able to perform the less than operation",
    function() {
      expect(4).toBeLessThan(5);
    });
```

```
    });

    describe("the toBeGreaterThan Matcher", function() {
        it("should be able to perform the greater than operation",
        function() {
          expect(5).toBeGreaterThan(4);
        });
    });
```

The toMatch matcher

The toMatch matcher is used to check whether a value matches a string or a regular expression. The following code snippet shows an example of the toMatch matcher, which ensures that the expect parameter is a digit:

```
    describe("the toMatch Matcher", function() {
        it("should be able to match the value with a regular expression",
        function() {
          expect(5).toMatch("[0-9]");
        });
    });
```

Developing custom Jasmine matchers

In addition to all of the mentioned built-in matchers, Jasmine enables you to develop custom matchers to have more powerful and descriptive testing code. Let's develop two custom matchers, toBePrimeNumber and toBeSumOf, to understand how to develop custom matchers in Jasmine.

The purpose of the toBePrimeNumber matcher is to check whether the actual number (the number in the expect function) is a prime number, while the toBeSumOf matcher checks whether the sum of its two arguments is equal to the actual number.

In order to define a custom matcher in Jasmine, you should use the addMatchers API to define the matcher(s) passing an object parameter to the API. The object parameter is represented as a set of key-value pairs. Every key in the object represents the matcher's name, while the value represents the matcher's associated function (the matcher's implementation). The definition of the matchers can be placed in either the beforeEach or the it block. The following code snippet shows the toBePrimeNumber and toBeSumOf custom matchers:

```
    beforeEach(function(){
      this.addMatchers({
          toBeSumOf: function (firstNumber, secondNumber) {
            return this.actual == firstNumber + secondNumber;
```

```
    },
    toBePrimeNumber: function() {
      if (this.actual < 2) {
      return false;
      }

      var n = Math.sqrt(this.actual);

      for (var i = 2; i <= n; ++i) {
      if (this.actual % i == 0) {
      return false;
      }
      }

      return true;
    }
  });
});
```

After defining the custom matchers, they can be used like the other built-in matchers in the test code, as shown in the following code snippet:

```
describe("Testing toBeSumOf custom matcher", function() {
  it("should be able to calculate the sum of two numbers",
  function() {
    expect(10).toBeSumOf(7, 3);
  });
});

describe("Testing toBePrimeNumber custom matcher", function() {
  it("should be able to know prime number", function() {
    expect(13).toBePrimeNumber();
  });

  it("should be able to know non-prime number", function() {
    expect(4).not.toBePrimeNumber();
  });
});
```

As shown in the preceding code snippet, you can use the not keyword with your defined custom matchers.

Testing asynchronous (Ajax) JavaScript code

Now, the question that comes to mind is how to test asynchronous (Ajax) JavaScript code using Jasmine. What was mentioned in the chapter so far is how to perform unit testing for synchronous JavaScript code. Jasmine fortunately includes powerful functions (`runs()`, `waits()`, and `waitsFor()`) for performing real Ajax testing (which requires the backend server to be up and running in order to complete the Ajax tests), and it also provides a mechanism for making fake Ajax testing (which does not require the availability of the backend server in order to complete the Ajax tests).

The runs() function

The code inside the `runs()` block runs directly as if it were outside the block. The main purpose of the `runs()` block is to work with the `waits()` and `waitsFor()` blocks to handle the testing of the asynchronous operations.

The `runs()` block has some characteristics that are important to know. The first point is that, if you have multiple `runs()` blocks in your spec, they will run sequentially, as shown in the following code snippet:

```
describe("Testing runs blocks", function() {
  it("should work correctly", function() {
    runs(function() {
      this.x = 1;
      expect(this.x).toEqual(1);
    });

    runs(function() {
      this.x++;
      expect(this.x).toEqual(2);
    });

    runs(function() {
      this.x = this.x * 4;
      expect(this.x).toEqual(8);
    });

  });
});
```

In the preceding code snippet, the `runs()` blocks run in sequence; when the first `runs()` block completes, the value of `this.x` is initialized to 1. Then, the second `runs()` block runs, and the value of `this.x` is incremented by 1 to be 2. Finally, the last `runs()` block runs, and the value of `this.x` is multiplied by 4 to be 8.

The second important point here is that the properties between the `runs()` blocks can be shared using the `this` keyword, as shown in the next code snippet.

The waits() function

The `waits()` function pauses the execution of the next block until its timeout period parameter is passed, in order to give the JavaScript code the opportunity to perform some other operations. The following code snippet shows an example of the `waits()` functionality with the `runs()` blocks:

```
describe("Testing waits with runs blocks", function() {
    it("should work correctly", function() {
        runs(function() {
            this.x = 1;

            var localThis = this;

            window.setTimeout(function() {
                localThis.x += 99;
            }, 500);
        });

        runs(function() {
            expect(this.x).toEqual(1);
        });

        waits(1000);

        runs(function() {
            expect(this.x).toEqual(100);
        });

    });
});
```

In the first `runs()` block, the `this.x` variable is set to 1 and a JavaScript `setTimeout` method is created to increment the `this.x` variable by 99 after 500 milliseconds. Before 500 milliseconds, the second `runs()` block verifies that `this.x` is equal to 1. Then, `waits(1000)` pauses the execution of the next `runs()` block by 1000 milliseconds, which is enough time for `setTimeout` to complete its execution and incrementing `this.x` by `99` to be `100`. After the `1000` milliseconds, the last `runs()` block verifies that the `this.x` variable is `100`.

In real applications, we may not know the exact time to wait for until the asynchronous operation completes its execution. Fortunately, Jasmine provides a more powerful mechanism to wait for the results of asynchronous operations, the `waitsFor()` function.

The waitsFor() function

The `waitsFor()` function provides a more powerful interface that can pause the execution of the next block until its provided function returns true or a specific timeout period passes. The following code snippet shows an example of the `waitsFor()` functionality with the `runs()` blocks:

```
describe("Testing waitsFor with runs blocks", function() {
  it("should work correctly", function() {
    runs(function() {
      this.x = 1;

      var localThis = this;

      var intervalID = window.setInterval(function() {
        localThis.x += 1;

        if (localThis.x == 100) {
          window.clearInterval(intervalID);
        }
      }, 20);
    });

    waitsFor(function() {
      return this.x == 100;
    }, "Something wrong happens, it should not wait all of this
    time", 5000);

    runs(function() {
      expect(this.x).toEqual(100);
    });

  });
});
```

In the first runs() block, the this.x variable is set to 1, and a JavaScript setInterval method is created to continuously increment the this.x variable with 1 every 20 milliseconds, and stop incrementing this.x once its value becomes 100; that is, after 2000 milliseconds are up, setInterval stops execution. Before 2000 milliseconds are complete, the second waitsFor() function pauses executing the next runs block until either this.x reaches 100 or the operation times out after 5000 milliseconds. After 2000 milliseconds, the value of this.x becomes 100, which results in a true condition result in the return of the waitsFor() provided function. This will result in executing the next runs block, which checks that this.x is equal to 100.

The waitsFor() function is mostly used for testing real Ajax requests; it waits for the completion of the execution of the Ajax callback with the help of Jasmine Spies.

 A Jasmine Spy is a replacement for a JavaScript function that can either be a callback, an instance method, a static method, or an object constructor.

The following code snippet shows how to test a real Ajax request:

```
describe("when waitsFor is used for testing real Ajax requests",
function() {
    it("should do this very well with the Jasmine Spy", function() {


        var successCallBack = jasmine.createSpy();
        var failureCallBack = jasmine.createSpy();

        asyncSystem.doAjaxOperation(inputData, successCallBack,
        failureCallBack);

        waitsFor(function() {
            return successCallBack.callCount > 0;
        }, "operation never completed", 10000);

        runs(function() {
            expect(successCallBack).toHaveBeenCalled();
            expect(failureCallBack).not.toHaveBeenCalled();
        });
    });


});
```

In the preceding code snippet, two Jasmine Spies are created using `jasmine.createSpy()` to replace the Ajax operation callbacks (the success callback and the failure callback), and then the asynchronous system is called with the input data and the success and failure callbacks (the two Jasmine Spies). The `waitsFor()` provided function waits for the calling of the success callback by using the `callCount` property of the spy. If the success callback is not called after `10000` milliseconds, the test fails.

 In addition to the `callCount` property, Jasmine Spy has two other properties. `mostRecentCall.args` returns an array of the arguments from the last call to the Spy and `argsForCall[i]` returns an array of the arguments from the call number `i` to the Spy.

Finally, the final `runs()` block ensures that the success callback is called using the spy matcher `toHaveBeenCalled()` (you can omit this line because it is already known that the success callback is called from the `waitsFor` provided function; however, I like to add this check for increasing the readability of the test) and ensures that the failure callback is not called using the `not` keyword with the `toHaveBeenCalled()` matcher.

 In addition to the `toHaveBeenCalled()` matcher, Jasmine Spies has another custom matcher, the `toHaveBeenCalledWith(arguments)` matcher, which checks if the spy is called with the specified arguments.

The spyOn() function

In the previous section, we learned how to create a spy using the `jasmine.createSpy()` API in order to replace the Ajax callbacks with the spies for making a complete real Ajax testing. The question that may come to mind now is whether it is possible to make a fake Ajax testing using Jasmine if there is no server available and you want to check that things will work correctly after the response comes from the server. (In other words, is it possible to mock the Ajax testing in Jasmine?) The answer to this question is yes. The Ajax fake testing can be simulated using the Jasmine `spyOn()` function, which can spy on the asynchronous operation and routes its calls to a fake function. First of all, let's see how `spyOn()` works. `spyOn()` can spy on a callback, an instance method, a static method, or an object constructor.

The following code snippet shows how `spyOn()` can spy on an instance method of the `SimpleMath` object:

```
SimpleMath = function() {
};

SimpleMath.prototype.getFactorial = function (number) {
    //...
}

describe("Testing spyOn", function() {
  it("should spy on instance methods", function() {
    var simpleMath = new SimpleMath();

    spyOn(simpleMath, 'getFactorial');
    simpleMath.getFactorial(3);

    expect(simpleMath.getFactorial).toHaveBeenCalledWith(3);
  });
});
```

The `spyOn()` method spies on the `getFactorial` method of the `SimpleMath` object. The `getFactorial` method of the `SimpleMath` object is called with number 3. Finally, the `simpleMath.getFactorial` spy knows that the instance method has been called with number 3 using the `toHaveBeenCalledWith` matcher.

> Spies are automatically removed after each spec. So make sure that you define them in the `beforeEach` function or within every spec separately.

In order to simulate the fake Ajax testing behavior, the spy has a powerful method, which is the `andCallFake(function)` method that calls its function parameter when the spy is called. The following code snippet shows you how to perform a fake Ajax testing using Jasmine:

```
describe("when making a fake Ajax testing", function() {
  it("should be done the Jasmine Spy and the andCallFake
      function", function() {
    var successCallBack = jasmine.createSpy();
    var failureCallBack = jasmine.createSpy();
    var successFakeData = "Succcess Fake Data ...";

    spyOn(asyncSystem,
    'doAjaxOperation').andCallFake(function(inputData,
    successCallBack, failureCallBack) {
      successCallBack(successFakeData);
    });
```

```
        asyncSystem.doAjaxOperation(inputData, successCallBack,
        failureCallBack);

        expect(successCallBack).toHaveBeenCalled();
        expect(failureCallBack).not.toHaveBeenCalled();
    });
});
```

A spy is created on the `doAjaxOperation` method of the `asyncSystem` object, and an order is given to the spy through the `andCallFake` method to call the fake function that has the same parameters of real `doAjaxOperation` when a call is done to original `asyncSystem.doAjaxOperation`. The fake function calls `successCallBack` to simulate a successful Ajax operation. After calling `asyncSystem.doAjaxOperation`, which does not go to the server anymore, thanks to the spy, as it executes the fake function, and finally `successCallBack` is checked that it has been called while `failureCallBack` is checked that it has never been called during the spec. Notice we are not using the `waits()`, `waitsFor()`, or `runs()` functions anymore in the fake testing because this test is fully performed on the client side so there is no need to wait for a response from the server.

 Besides the `andCallFake(function)` method, there are other three useful methods in the spy that you may use. The first one is the `andCallThrough()` method, which calls the original function that the spy spied on when the spy was called. The second one is the `andReturn(arguments)` method, which returns the arguments parameter when the spy is called. Finally, the `andThrow(exception)` method throws an exception when the spy is called.

HTML fixtures

HTML fixtures are the input HTML code that is needed for executing one or more tests that require manipulating Document Object Model (DOM) elements. Jasmine does not provide an API for handling HTML fixtures in the specs. However, fortunately, there are some extensions of the framework that provide this functionality. One of the best plugins that provide this functionality is the `jasmine-jquery` plugin. Although `jasmine-jquery` goes beyond the HTML fixtures loading (it has a powerful set of matchers for the jQuery framework), I will focus only on its HTML fixture functionality, as this is what we need as JavaScript developers from Jasmine in order to test our JavaScript applications even though the applications are using a JavaScript library such as Dojo or jQuery or are not using any JavaScript library at all.

Configuring the jasmine-jquery plugin

In order to configure the `jasmine-jquery` plugin with Jasmine we need to perform the following steps:

1. Download the plugin ZIP file from `https://github.com/velesin/ jasmine-jquery/downloads`.

2. Unpack the `velesin-jasmine-jquery.zip` (at the time of writing this chapter, the version of `jasmine-jquery` plugin was 1.3.2).

3. Get the `jasmine-jquery.js` file from the `lib` folder, and the `jquery.js` file from the `vendor\jquery` folder.

4. Group the `jasmine-jquery.js` and `jquery.js` files under a folder. Let's make the folder name `jasmine-jquery`. I usually place the `jasmine-jquery` folder under a `plugins` folder in the `lib` folder of Jasmine. The following screenshot shows the structure of the Jasmine tests in the weather application:

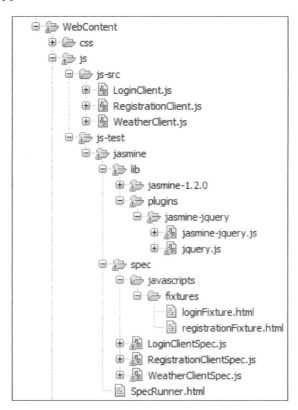

5. Finally, include the two files in the `SpecRunner.html` file as shown in the highlighted lines of the following code snippet:

```
<script type="text/javascript" src="lib/jasmine-
1.2.0/jasmine.js"></script>
<script type="text/javascript" src="lib/jasmine-
1.2.0/jasmine-html.js"></script>

<!-- The plugin files -->
<script type="text/javascript" src="lib/plugins/jasmine-
jquery/jquery.js"></script>
<script type="text/javascript" src="lib/plugins/jasmine-
jquery/jasmine-jquery.js"></script>

<!-- include spec files here... -->
...
```

The loadFixtures module

This fixture module of `jasmine-jquery` allows loading the HTML content to be used by the tests. Simply, you can put the fixtures you want to load for your tests in the `spec\javascripts\fixtures` conventional folder and use the `loadFixtures` API to load the fixture(s). The following code snippet shows an example of the `loadFixtures` module:

```
beforeEach(function() {
    loadFixtures("registrationFixture.html");
});
```

In the `spec\javascripts\fixtures` folder, the `registrationFixture.html` file is as shown in the following code snippet:

```
<label for="username">Username (Email)  <span id="usernameMessage"
class="error"></span></label>
<input type="text" id="username" name="username"/>

<label for="password1">Password  <span id="passwordMessage1"
class="error"></span></label>
<input type="password" id="password1" name="password1"/>

<label for="password2">Confirm your password</label>
<input type="password" id="password2" name="password2"/>
```

You can change the default fixtures path instead of working with the `spec\javascripts\fixtures` conventional folder using:

```
jasmine.getFixtures().fixturesPath = '[The new path]';
```

The `loadFixtures` API can be used for loading multiple fixtures for the same test. You can use the `loadFixtures` API as follows:

```
loadFixtures(fixtureUrl [, fixtureUrl, ...])
```

Once you use the `loadFixtures` API to load the fixture(s), the fixture is loaded in the `<div id="jasmine-fixtures"></div>` container and added to the DOM using the fixture module. Fixtures are automatically cleaned up between tests so you do not have to clean them up manually. For speeding up the tests, `jasmine-jquery` makes an internal caching for the HTML fixtures in order to avoid the overhead if you decide to load the same fixture file many times in the tests.

The `loadFixtures(...)` API is a shortcut for the `jasmine.getFixtures().load(...)` so you can freely use any of them to load the HTML fixtures for the tests.

In `jasmine-jquery` you have the option to write the HTML code inline without having to load it from an external file. You can do this using the `jasmine.getFixtures().set(...)` API as follows:

```
jasmine.getFixtures().set('<div id="someDiv">HTML code ...</div>');
```

While testing the weather application, both the `load` and `set` APIs will be used for loading the test fixtures.

I recommend using the inline approach if the HTML fixture is a few lines of HTML code. However, if the HTML fixture is large, then it is better to load it from an external file in order to have a better readable testing code.

This is all what we need to know from `jasmine-jquery` in order to load the needed fixtures for our tests. The next step is to write the Jasmine tests for the weather application.

Testing the weather application

Now, we come to write the Jasmine tests for our weather application. Actually, after you know how to write Jasmine tests for both synchronous and asynchronous JavaScript code and how to load the HTML fixtures in your Jasmine tests from the previous sections, testing the weather application is an easy task. As you may remember we have three major JavaScript objects in the weather application that we need to write unit tests for: the `LoginClient`, `RegistrationClient`, and `WeatherClient` objects.

One of the best practices that I recommend is to separate the JavaScript source and testing code as shown in the preceding screenshot. There are two parent folders, one for the JavaScript source, which I call `js-src` folder, and the other for the JavaScript tests, which I call `js-test` folder. The `js-test` folder contains the tests written by the testing frameworks that will be used in this book; for now, it contains a `jasmine` folder that includes the Jasmine tests.

As indicated in the *Configuration* section, Jasmine structure can be modified to fulfill the organization of every web application. The preceding screenshot shows the customized Jasmine structure for our weather application, under the `jasmine` folder; we have two subfolders, the `spec` and the `lib` folders, while the `src` folder is now represented in the `js-src` folder, which is directly under the `js` folder.

The following code snippet shows the JavaScript files included for the Jasmine files, the jasmine-jquery files, the spec files, and the source files in the `SpecRunner.html` of the weather application according to the preceding screenshot:

```html
<!-- The Jasmine files -->
<link rel="shortcut icon" type="image/png" href="lib/jasmine-1.2.0/
jasmine_favicon.png">
<link rel="stylesheet" type="text/css" href="lib/jasmine-1.2.0/
jasmine.css">
<script type="text/javascript" src="lib/jasmine-1.2.0/jasmine.js"></
script>
<script type="text/javascript" src="lib/jasmine-1.2.0/jasmine-html.
js"></script>

<!-- The jasmine-jquery files -->
<script type="text/javascript" src="lib/plugins/jasmine-jquery/jquery.
js"></script>
<script type="text/javascript" src="lib/plugins/jasmine-jquery/
jasmine-jquery.js"></script>

<!-- include spec files here... -->
<script type="text/javascript" src="spec/LoginClientSpec.js"></script>
<script type="text/javascript" src="spec/RegistrationClientSpec.js"></
```

```
script>
<script type="text/javascript" src="spec/WeatherClientSpec.js"></
script>

<!-- include source files here... -->
<script type="text/javascript" src="../../js-src/LoginClient.js"></
script>
<script type="text/javascript" src="../../js-src/RegistrationClient.
js"></script>
<script type="text/javascript" src="../../js-src/WeatherClient.js"></
script>
```

Testing the LoginClient object

In the LoginClient object, we will unit test the following functionalities:

- Validation of empty username and password
- Validating that the username is in e-mail address format
- Validating that the password contains at least one digit, one capital and small letter, at least one special character, and six characters or more

The following code snippet shows the first test suite of LoginClientSpec, which tests the validation of empty username and password:

```
describe("LoginClientSpec", function() {
    var loginClient;
    var loginForm;

    beforeEach(function() {
      loadFixtures("loginFixture.html");

      loginClient = new weatherapp.LoginClient();

      loginForm = {
          "userNameField" : "username",
          "passwordField" : "password",
          "userNameMessage" : "usernameMessage",
          "passwordMessage" : "passwordMessage"
      };
    });

  describe("when validating empty username and password",
  function() {
      it("should be able to display an error message when username
          is not entered", function() {
```

```
            document.getElementById("username").value = ""; /* setting
            username to empty */
            document.getElementById("password").value = "Admin@123";

            loginClient.validateLoginForm(loginForm);

            expect(document.getElementById("usernameMessage").innerHTML).
            toEqual("(field is required)");
        });

        it("should be able to display an error message when password
        is not entered", function() {
            document.getElementById("username").value =
            "someone@yahoo.com";
            document.getElementById("password").value = "";    /*
            setting password to empty */

            loginClient.validateLoginForm(loginForm);

            expect(document.getElementById("passwordMessage").innerHTML).
    toEqual("(field is required)");
        });
    });
    //...
});
```

In the preceding code snippet, beforeEach loads the HTML fixture of the login
client test, creates an instance from weatherapp.LoginClient, and creates the
loginForm object, which holds the IDs of the login form that will be used in the test.
The following code snippet shows the HTML fixture of the login client test in the
loginFixture.html file:

```
<label for="username">Username  <span id="usernameMessage"
class="error"></span></label>
<input type="text" id="username" name="username"/>
<label for="password">Password  <span id="passwordMessage"
class="error"></span></label>
<input type="password" id="password" name="password"/>
```

The first spec tests that the LoginClient object should be able to display an error
message when username is not entered. It sets an empty value in the "username"
field and then calls the validateLoginForm API of the LoginClient object. Finally,
it checks that the validateLoginForm API produces the "(field is required)"
message in the username message field. The second spec is doing the same thing but
with the password field, not with the username field.

The following code snippet shows the second and the third test suites of `LoginClientSpec`, which validates the formats of the username and password fields:

```
describe("when validating username format", function() {
    it("should be able to display an error message when username
      format is not correct", function() {
    document.getElementById("username").value = "someone@yahoo";
    /* setting username to incorrect format */
    document.getElementById("password").value = "Admin@123";

    loginClient.validateLoginForm(loginForm);

    expect(document.getElementById("usernameMessage").innerHTML).
    toEqual("(format is invalid)");
    });
});

describe("when validating password format", function() {
    it("should be able to display an error message when
      password format is not correct", function() {
    document.getElementById("username").value =
    "someone@yahoo.com";
    document.getElementById("password").value = "admin@123";
    /* setting password to incorrect format */

    loginClient.validateLoginForm(loginForm);

    expect(document.getElementById("passwordMessage").innerHTML).
    toEqual("(format is invalid)");
    });
});
```

In the preceding code snippet, the first suite tests the validation of the username format. It tests that the `LoginClient` object should be able to display an error message when the username format is not correct. It sets an invalid e-mail value in the `"username"` field and then calls the `validateLoginForm` API of the `LoginClient` object. Finally, it checks that the `validateLoginForm` API produces the `"(format is invalid)"` message in the username message field.

The second suite does the same thing but with the password field not with the username field. It enters a password that does not comply with the application's password rules; it enters a password that does not include a capital letter, and then calls the `validateLoginForm` API of the `LoginClient` object. Finally, it checks that the `validateLoginForm` API produces the `"(format is invalid)"` message in the password message field.

It may not be always suitable while performing JavaScript unit testing to test against the application messages because the application messages can change at any time. However, in the weather application testing example, I performed testing on the application messages in order to show you how to perform testing against the HTML DOM elements. If you want to avoid testing against DOM elements, you can test against the `validateLoginForm` API directly as follows:

```
expect(loginClient.validateLoginForm(loginForm)).
toEqual(true);
```

Testing the RegistrationClient object

In the `RegistrationClient` object, we will test the following functionalities:

- Validation of empty username and password
- Validation of matched passwords
- Validating that the username is in e-mail address format
- Validating that the password contains at least one digit, one capital and small letter, at least one special character, and six characters or more
- Validating that the user registration Ajax functionality is performed correctly

The first four points will not be explained because they are pretty similar to the tests that are explained in `LoginClientSpec`, so let's explain how to check that the user registration functionality is done correctly. The following code snippet shows the user registration test scenarios:

```
describe("RegistrationClientSpec", function() {
    var registrationClient;
    var registrationForm;
    var userName;

    beforeEach(function() {
        loadFixtures("registrationFixture.html");

        registrationClient = new weatherapp.RegistrationClient();

      registrationForm = {
          "userNameField" : "username",
          "passwordField1" : "password1",
          "passwordField2" : "password2",
          "userNameMessage" : "usernameMessage",
          "passwordMessage1" : "passwordMessage1"
      };
```

```
  });

//The user registration test scenarios

describe("when user registration is done", function() {
  it("should be able to register valid user correctly",
  function() {
    userName = "hazems" + new Date().getTime() + "@apache.org";

    document.getElementById("username").value = userName;
    document.getElementById("password1").value = "Admin@123";
    document.getElementById("password2").value = "Admin@123";

     var successCallBack = jasmine.createSpy();
     var failureCallBack = jasmine.createSpy();

     registrationClient.registerUser(registrationForm,
     successCallBack, failureCallBack);

     waitsFor(function() {
         return successCallBack.callCount > 0;
       }, "registration never completed", 10000);

     runs(function() {
         expect(successCallBack).toHaveBeenCalled();
         expect(failureCallBack).not.toHaveBeenCalled();
       });
  });

  it("should fail when a specific user id is already
  registered", function() {
    document.getElementById("username").value = userName;
    document.getElementById("password1").value = "Admin@123";
    document.getElementById("password2").value = "Admin@123";

    var successCallBack = jasmine.createSpy();
    var failureCallBack = jasmine.createSpy();

    registrationClient.registerUser(registrationForm,
    successCallBack, failureCallBack);

    waitsFor(function() {
        return failureCallBack.callCount > 0;
      }, "registration never completed", 10000);
```

```
        runs(function() {
                expect(failureCallBack).toHaveBeenCalled();
            expect(failureCallBack.mostRecentCall.args[0].xmlhttp.
    responseText, "A user with the same username is already registered
    ...");
                expect(successCallBack).not.toHaveBeenCalled();
            });
        });


        });
    });
```

In the preceding code snippet, `beforeEach` loads the fixture of the registration client test, creates an instance from `weatherapp.RegistrationClient`, and creates the `registrationForm` object, which holds the IDs of the registration form that will be used in the test. The following code snippet shows the fixture of the registration client test in the `registrationFixture.html` file:

```
<label for="username">Username (Email)   <span id="usernameMessage"
class="error"></span></label>
<input type="text" id="username" name="username"/>

<label for="password1">Password   <span id="passwordMessage1"
class="error"></span></label>
<input type="password" id="password1" name="password1"/>

<label for="password2">Confirm your password</label>
<input type="password" id="password2" name="password2"/>
```

The registration testing suite has two main test scenarios:

- The registration client should be able to register valid user correctly
- The registration client should fail when registering a user ID that is already registered

In the first spec, the registration form is filled with a valid username and valid matched passwords; then two spies are created. The first spy replaces the success callback while the second one replaces the failure callback. `registrationClient.registerUser` is called with the registration form, the success callback, and the failure callback parameters and the `waitsFor()` function waits for a call to the success callback or it will be timed out after `10000` milliseconds. Once `waitsFor()` is completed, the `runs` block checks that the success callback is called and the failure callback is not called for ensuring that the registration operation is completed correctly.

Note that the Ajax testing of the weather application is real Ajax testing; this requires the server to be up and running in order to perform the test correctly. If you want to make fake Ajax testing, for example, for the successful user registration, you can do this as you learned from the spyOn section as follows:

```
it("makes a fake registration Ajax call", function() {
        document.getElementById("username").value = userName;
        document.getElementById("password1").value = "Admin@123";
        document.getElementById("password2").value = "Admin@123";
        var successCallBack = jasmine.createSpy();
        var failureCallBack = jasmine.createSpy();

        spyOn(registrationClient,
        'registerUser').andCallFake(function(registrationForm,
        successCallBack, failureCallBack) {
          successCallBack();
          });

        registrationClient.registerUser(registrationForm,
        successCallBack, failureCallBack);

        expect(successCallBack).toHaveBeenCalled();
        expect(failureCallBack).not.toHaveBeenCalled();

      });
```

In the second spec, the registration form is filled with the same username that is already registered in the first spec and then two spies are created. The first spy replaces the success callback while the second one replaces the failure callback. registrationClient.registerUser is called with the registration form, the success callback, and the failure callback parameters and the waitsFor() function waits for a call to the failure callback or it will be timed out after 10000 milliseconds. Once waitsFor() is completed, the runs block checks that the failure callback is called, and using expect(failureCallBack.mostRecentCall.args[0].xmlhttp. responseText, "A user with the same username is already registered ...") ensures that the server sends the correct duplicate registration failure message to the failure callback. Finally, the spec checks that the success callback is not called for ensuring that the registration operation is not done because of the already registered user ID. This was all about the registration tests.

Testing the WeatherClient object

In the `WeatherClient` object, we will test the following functionalities:

- Getting the weather of a valid location

- Getting the weather for an invalid location (the system should display an error message for this case)

For testing the `WeatherClient` object, the same technique that we used in the `registerUser` test case is followed. I will leave this test for you as an exercise; you can get the full source code of the `WeatherClientSpec.js` file from the `Chapter 2` folder in the code bundle available from the book's website.

Running the weather application tests

In order to run the weather application tests correctly, you have to make sure that the server is up and running in order to pass the Ajax test suites. So, you need to deploy this chapter's updated version of the weather application on Tomcat 6 as explained in *Chapter 1, Unit Testing JavaScript Applications* and then type in the browser the following URL to see the passing tests:

```
http://localhost:8080[or other Tomcat port]/weatherApplication/js/js-
test/jasmine/SpecRunner.html
```

Summary

In this chapter, you learned what Jasmine is and how to use it for testing synchronous JavaScript code. You also learned how to test asynchronous (Ajax) JavaScript code using Jasmine Spies and the `waitsFor`/`runs` mechanism. You also learned how to make fake Ajax testing using Jasmine. You learned the various matchers provided by the framework, and know how to load the HTML fixtures easily in your Jasmine tests. Finally, I explained how to apply all of these things for testing the weather application using Jasmine. In the next chapter, you will learn how to work with the YUI Test framework and how to use it for testing the weather application.

3
YUI Test

YUI Test is one of the most popular JavaScript unit testing frameworks. Although YUI Test is part of the **Yahoo! User Interface (YUI)** JavaScript library (YUI is an open source JavaScript and CSS library that can be used to build Rich Internet Applications), it can be used to test any independent JavaScript code that does not use the YUI library. YUI Test provides a simple syntax for creating JavaScript test cases that can run either from the browser or from the command line; it also provides a clean mechanism for testing asynchronous (Ajax) JavaScript code. If you are familiar with the syntax of **xUnit** frameworks (such as JUnit), you will find yourself familiar with the YUI Test syntax. In this chapter, the framework will be illustrated in detail and will be used to test the weather application that is discussed in *Chapter 1, Unit Testing JavaScript Applications.*

In YUI Test, there are different ways to display test results. You can display the test results in the browser console or develop your custom test runner pages to display the test results. It is preferable to develop custom test runner pages in order to display the test results in all the browsers because some browsers do not support the `console` object. The `console` object is supported in Firefox with Firebug installed, Safari 3+, Internet Explorer 8+, and Chrome.

Before writing your first YUI test, you need to know the structure of a custom YUI test runner page. We will create the test runner page, `BasicRunner.html`, that will be the basis for all the test runner pages used in this chapter. In order to build the test runner page, first of all you need to include the YUI JavaScript file `yui-min.js`—from the Yahoo! Content Delivery Network (CDN)—in the `BasicRunner.html` file, as follows:

```
<script src="http://yui.yahooapis.com/3.6.0/build/yui/yui-min.js"></
script>
```

At the time of this writing, the latest version of YUI Test is 3.6.0, which is the one used in this chapter. After including the YUI JavaScript file, we need to create and configure a YUI instance using the `YUI().use` API, as follows:

```
YUI().use('test', 'console', function(Y) {
    ...
});
```

The `YUI().use` API takes the list of YUI modules to be loaded. For the purpose of testing, we need the YUI `'test'` and `'console'` modules (the `'test'` module is responsible for creating the tests, while the `'console'` module is responsible for displaying the test results in a nifty console component). Then, the `YUI().use` API takes the test's callback function that is called *asynchronously* once the modules are loaded. The `Y` parameter in the callback function represents the YUI instance.

As shown in the following code snippet taken from the `BasicRunner.html` file, you can write the tests in the provided callback and then create a console component using the `Y.Console` object:

```
<HTML>
  <HEAD>
    <TITLE>YUITest Example</TITLE>
    <meta http-equiv="Content-Type" content="text/html;
    charset=utf-8">
    <script src="http://yui.yahooapis.com/3.6.0/build/yui/yui-
    min.js"></script>
  </HEAD>
  <BODY>
    <div id="log" class="yui3-skin-sam" style="margin:0px"></div>

    <script>

    // create a new YUI instance and populate it with the required
    modules.
    YUI().use('test', 'console', function(Y) {

      // Here write your test suites with the test cases
      (tests)...

      //create the console
      var console = new Y.Console({
        style: 'block',
        newestOnTop : false
      });
      console.render('#log');
```

```
    // Here run the tests

  });
  </script>


  </BODY>
</HTML>
```

The `console` object is rendered as a block element by setting the `style` attribute to `'block'`, and the results within the console can be displayed in the sequence of their executions by setting the `newestOnTop` attribute to `false`. Finally, the console component is created on the `log` div element.

Now you can run the tests, and they will be displayed automatically by the YUI console component. The following screenshot shows the `BasicRunner.html` file's console component without any developed tests:

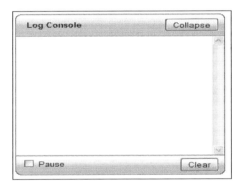

Writing your first YUI test

The YUI test can contain test suites, test cases, and test functions. A YUI test suite is a group of related test cases. Each test case includes one or more test functions for the JavaScript code. Every test function should contain one or more assertion in order to perform the tests and verify the outputs.

The YUI `Test.Suite` object is responsible for creating a YUI test suite, while the YUI `Test.Case` object creates a YUI test case. The `add` method of the `Test.Suite` object is used for attaching the test case object to the test suite. The following code snippet shows an example of a YUI test suite:

```
YUI().use('test', 'console', function(Y){
  var testcase1 = new Y.Test.Case({
```

```
    name: "testcase1",

    testFunction1: function() {
      //...
    },
    testFunction2: function() {
      //...
    }
  });

  var testcase2 = new Y.Test.Case({
    name: "testcase2",

    testAnotherFunction: function() {
      //...
    }
  });

  var suite = new Y.Test.Suite("Testsuite");

  suite.add(testcase1);
  suite.add(testcase2);

  //...
});
```

As shown in the preceding code snippet, two test cases are created. The first test case is named `testcase1`; it contains two test functions, `testFunction1` and `testFunction2`. In YUI Test, you can create a test function simply by starting the function name with the word "test". The second test case is named `testcase2`; and it contains a single test function, `testAnotherFunction`. A test suite is created with the name `Testsuite`. Finally, `testcase1` and `testcase2` are added to the `Testsuite` test suite. In YUI Test, you have the option of creating a friendly test name for the test function, as follows:

```
var testCase = new Y.Test.Case({
    name: "some Testcase",
    "The test should do X": function () {
        //...
    },
    "The test should do Y": function () {
        //...
    }
});
```

The "some Testcase" test case contains two tests with the names "The test should do X" and "The test should do Y".

Let's now move to testing the SimpleMath JavaScript object (which we tested using Jasmine in *Chapter 2, Jasmine*). The following code snippet reminds you with the code of the SimpleMath object:

```
SimpleMath = function() {
};

SimpleMath.prototype.getFactorial = function (number) {

  if (number < 0) {
    throw new Error("There is no factorial for negative numbers");
  }
  else if (number == 1 || number == 0) {

    // If number <= 1 then number! = 1.
      return 1;
  } else {

    // If number > 1 then number! = number * (number-1)!
      return number * this.getFactorial(number-1);
  }
}

SimpleMath.prototype.signum = function (number) {
    if (number > 0)  {
    return 1;
  } else if (number == 0) {
    return 0;
  } else {
    return -1;
  }
}

SimpleMath.prototype.average = function (number1, number2) {
    return (number1 + number2) / 2;
}
```

As we did in *Chapter 2, Jasmine*, we will develop the following three test scenarios for the getFactorial method:

- A positive number
- Zero
- A negative number

The following code snippet shows how to test calculating the factorial of a positive number (3), 0, and a negative number (-10) using YUI Test:

```
YUI().use('test', 'console', function(Y){
  var factorialTestcase = new Y.Test.Case({
    name: "Factorial Testcase",

    _should: {
      error: {
        testNegativeNumber: true //this test should throw an error
      }
    },

    setUp: function() {
      this.simpleMath = new SimpleMath();
    },
    tearDown: function() {
      delete this.simpleMath;
    },
    testPositiveNumber: function() {
      Y.Assert.areEqual(6, this.simpleMath.getFactorial(3));
    },
    testZero: function() {
      Y.Assert.areEqual(1, this.simpleMath.getFactorial(0));
    },
    testNegativeNumber: function() {
      this.simpleMath.getFactorial(-10);
    }
  });

  //...

});
```

The Y.Test.Case object declares a new test case called "Factorial Testcase". The setUp method is used to initialize the test functions in the test case; that is, the setUp method is called once before the run of each test function in the test case.

In the `setUp` method, the `simpleMath` object is created using `new SimpleMath()`. The `tearDown` method is used to de-initialize the test functions in the test case; the `tearDown` method is called once after the run of each test function in the test case. In the factorial tests, the `tearDown` method is used to clean up resources by deleting the created `simpleMath` object.

In the first test function of the `getFactorial` test case, the `Y.Assert.areEqual` assertion function calls `simpleMath.getFactorial(3)` and expects the result to be 6. If `simpleMath.getFactorial(3)` returns a value other than 6, the test fails. We have many other assertions to use instead of `Y.Assert.areEqual`; we shall be discussing them in more detail in the *Assertions* section.

In the second test function of the `getFactorial` test case, the `Y.Assert.areEqual` assertion function calls `simpleMath.getFactorial(0)` and expects it to be equal to 1. In the last test function of the `getFactorial` test case, the `Y.Assert.areEqual` assertion function calls `simpleMath.getFactorial(-10)` and expects it to throw an error by using the `_should.error` object. In YUI Test, if you set a property whose name is the test method's name and value is `true` in the `_should.error` object, this means that this test method must throw an error in order to have the test function pass.

After finalizing the `getFactorial` test case, we come to a new test case that tests the functionality of the `signum` method provided by the `SimpleMath` object. The following code snippet shows the signum test case:

```
var signumTestcase = new Y.Test.Case({
  name: "Signum Testcase",

  setUp: function() {
    this.simpleMath = new SimpleMath();
  },
  tearDown: function() {
    delete this.simpleMath;
  },
  testPositiveNumber: function() {
    Y.Assert.areEqual(1, this.simpleMath.signum(3));
  },
  testZero: function() {
    Y.Assert.areEqual(0, this.simpleMath.signum(0));
  },
  testNegativeNumber: function() {
    Y.Assert.areEqual(-1, this.simpleMath.signum(-1000));
  }
});
```

In the preceding code snippet, we have three tests for the `signum` method:

- The first test is about getting the signum value for a positive number (3)
- The second test is about getting the signum value for 0
- The last test is about getting the signum value for a negative number (-1000)

The following code snippet shows the average test case:

```
var averageTestcase = new Y.Test.Case({
  name: "Average Testcase",

  setUp: function() {
    this.simpleMath = new SimpleMath();
  },
  tearDown: function() {
    delete this.simpleMath;
  },
  testAverage: function() {
    Y.Assert.areEqual(4.5, this.simpleMath.average(3, 6));
  }
});
```

In the average test case, the `testAverage` test function ensures that the average is calculated correctly by calling the `average` method, using the two parameters 3 and 6, and expecting the result to be 4.5.

In the following code snippet, a test suite `"SimpleMath Test Suite"` is created in order to group the test cases `factorialTestcase`, `signumTestcase`, and `averageTestcase`. Finally, the `console` component is created to display the test results.

```
var suite = new Y.Test.Suite("SimpleMath Test Suite");

suite.add(factorialTestcase);
suite.add(signumTestcase);
suite.add(averageTestcase);

//create the console
var console = new Y.Console({
  style: 'block',
  newestOnTop : false
});
console.render('#resultsPanel');

Y.Test.Runner.add(suite);
Y.Test.Runner.run();
```

In order to run the test suite, we need to add it to the YUI test runner page by using the `Y.Test.Runner.add` API, and then run the YUI test runner page by using the `Y.Test.Runner.run` API. After clicking the `SimpleMath` YUI test page `SimpleMathTests.html`, you will find the test results, as shown in the following screenshot:

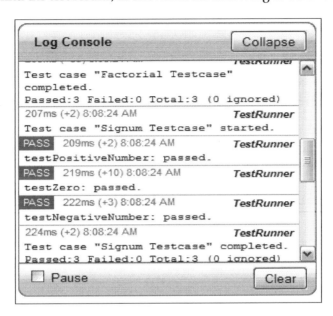

Finally, the following code snippet shows the complete structure of the `SimpleMath` YUI test page, which includes the `simpleMath.js` source file to be tested in the page:

```
<HTML>
  <HEAD>
    <TITLE>SimpleMathTest</TITLE>
    <meta http-equiv="Content-Type" content="text/html;
    charset=utf-8">
    <script src="http://yui.yahooapis.com/3.6.0/build/yui/yui-
    min.js"></script>
    <script src="src/simpleMath.js"></script>

  </HEAD>
  <BODY>
    <div id="resultsPanel" class="yui3-skin-sam"></div>
    <script language="javascript" type="text/javascript">
    YUI().use('test', 'console', function(Y){
      var factorialTestcase = new Y.Test.Case({

        ...

      });
```

```
        var signumTestcase = new Y.Test.Case({
...
        });

        var averageTestcase = new Y.Test.Case({
        ...
        });

        var suite = new Y.Test.Suite("SimpleMath Test Suite");

        suite.add(factorialTestcase);
        suite.add(signumTestcase);
        suite.add(averageTestcase);

        //create the console and run the test suite ...

    });
    </script>
  </BODY>
</HTML>
```

 It is recommended that you separate the test logic from the test runner file(s), that is, have the tests in separate JavaScript files and then include them in the test runner file(s). However, the test logic is embedded in the test runner file in the `simpleMath` testing example, for simplicity. In the *Testing the weather application* section, this sort of separation will be applied.

Assertions

An assertion is a function that validates a condition if the condition is not valid; it throws an error that causes the test to fail. A test method can include one or more assertions; all the assertions have to pass in order that the test method passes. In the first YUI test example, we used the `Y.Assert.areEqual` assertion. In this section, the other different built-in assertions provided by YUI Test will be illustrated.

The assert assertion

The `assert` function takes two parameters. The first parameter is a condition, and the second parameter represents a failure message. It is passed if the condition is true, and when it fails, the failure message is displayed. For example:

```
Y.assert(10 == 10, "Error ..."); // will pass
Y.assert(10 != 10, "Error ..."); // will fail and display an error
```

The areEqual and areNotEqual assertions

The `areEqual` assertion function takes three parameters; the first two parameters represent the expected and actual values, and the third parameter is optional and represents a failure message. The `areEqual` function is passed if the actual is equal to the expected. If they are not equal, the test fails and the optional failure message is displayed. The `areNotEqual` function ensures that the actual and expected parameters are not equal.

It is very important to know that the `areEqual` and `areNotEqual` functions are using the JavaScript `==` operator to perform the comparison, that is, they do the comparison and neglect the types. For example, the following assertions will pass:

```
Y.Assert.areEqual(10, 10, "10 should equal 10...");
Y.Assert.areEqual(10, "10", "10 should equal '10'...");
Y.Assert.areNotEqual(10, 11, "10 should not equal 11...");
```

The areSame and areNotSame assertions

The `areSame` and `areNotSame` assertion functions are much similar to the `areEqual` and `areNotEqual` assertions. The main difference between them is that the `areSame` and `areNotSame` assertion functions use the `===` operator for comparison, that is, they compare both the values and the types of the actual and expected parameters. For example, the following assertions will pass:

```
Y.Assert.areSame(10, 10, "10 is the same as 10...");
Y.Assert.areNotSame(10, 11, "10 is not the same as 11...");
Y.Assert.areNotSame(15, "15", "15 is not the same as '15'...");
Y.Assert.areNotSame(15, "16", "15 is not the same as '16'...");
```

The datatype assertions

The following set of assertion functions in YUI Test checks the value types. Each one of these assertion functions takes two parameters; the first parameter is the value to test and the second parameter is an optional failure message:

- `isBoolean()` is passed if the value is a Boolean
- `isString()` is passed if the value is a string
- `isNumber()` is passed if the value is a number
- `isArray()` is passed if the value is an array

- `isFunction()` is passed if the value is a function
- `isObject()` is passed if the value is an object

For example, the following assertions will pass:

```
Y.Assert.isBoolean(false);
Y.Assert.isString("some string");
Y.Assert.isNumber(1000);
Y.Assert.isArray([1, 2, 3]);
Y.Assert.isFunction(function(){ alert('test'); });
Y.Assert.isObject({somekey: 'someValue'});
```

YUI Test also provides generic assertion functions, `isTypeOf` and `isInstanceOf`, to check the datatypes.

The `isTypeOf()` method uses the JavaScript `typeof` operator in order to check the value type. It takes three parameters; the first parameter represents the value type, the second represents the value to test, and the third parameter is optional and represents a failure message. For example, the following `isTypeOf` assertions will pass:

```
Y.Assert.isTypeOf("boolean", false);
Y.Assert.isTypeOf("string", "some string");
Y.Assert.isTypeOf("number", 1000);
Y.Assert.isTypeOf("object", [1, 2, 3]);
Y.Assert.isTypeOf("function", function(){ alert('test'); });
Y.Assert.isTypeOf("object", {somekey: 'someValue'});
```

In addition to all of this, you can use the `isInstanceOf` assertion, which uses the JavaScript `instanceof` operator in order to check the value instance. It takes three parameters; the first parameter represents the type constructor, the second represents the value to test, and the third parameter is optional and represents a failure message.

Special value assertions

The following set of assertion functions in YUI Test checks whether a variable value belongs to one of the special values as mentioned in the following list. Each one of these functions takes two parameters; the first parameter is the value to test, and the second parameter is an optional failure message:

- `isUndefined()` is passed if the value is undefined
- `isNotUndefined()` is passed if the value is not undefined (defined)
- `isNull()` is passed if the value is null
- `isNotNull()` is passed if the value is not null
- `isNaN()` is passed if the value is not a number (NaN)

- isNotNaN() is passed if the value is not NaN
- isFalse() is passed if the value is false
- isTrue() is passed if the value is true

For example, the following assertions will pass:

```
this.someStr = "some string";
Y.Assert.isUndefined(this.anyUndefinedThing);
Y.Assert.isNotUndefined(this.someStr);
Y.Assert.isNull(null);
Y.Assert.isNotNull(this.someStr);
Y.Assert.isNaN(1000 / "string_value");
Y.Assert.isNotNaN(1000);
Y.Assert.isFalse(false);
Y.Assert.isTrue(true);
```

The fail assertion

In some situations, you may need to fail the test manually, for example, if you want to make your own custom assertion function that encapsulates specific validation logic. In order to do this, YUI Test provides the fail() method to fail the test manually. The Y.Assert.isAverage assertion is an example of a custom assertion that uses the fail() method:

```
Y.Assert.isAverage = function(number1, number2, expected,
failureMessage) {
  var actual = (number1 + number2) / 2;
  if (actual != expected) {
    Y.Assert.fail(failureMessage);
  }
}
```

The Y.Assert.isAverage custom assertion can be called by simply using the following code:

```
Y.Assert.isAverage(3, 4, 3.5, "Average is incorrect");
```

 The fail() method has an optional message parameter that is displayed when the fail() method is called.

Testing asynchronous (Ajax) JavaScript code

The common question that comes to mind is how to test asynchronous (Ajax) JavaScript code using YUI Test. What was mentioned earlier in this chapter so far is how to perform unit testing for synchronous JavaScript code. YUI Test provides two main APIs in order to perform real Ajax testing: `wait()` and `resume()`. Although the provided APIs of the YUI Test to perform real Ajax testing are not as rich as Jasmine (the provided YUI Test APIs do not, for example include something like spies or the Jasmine's automatic `waitsFor` mechanism), they are enough to perform a real Ajax test. Let me show you how to do this.

The wait and resume functions

The `wait()` function has two modes of operation. Its first mode pauses the execution of the test until its timeout period passes. For example:

```
this.wait(function() {
    Y.Assert.isAverage(3, 4, 3.5, "Average is incorrect");
}, 1000);
```

This code pauses the test for `1000` milliseconds, and after that its function in the first argument is executed.

The second mode of operation pauses the execution of the test until it is resumed using the `resume()` function; if it is not resumed using the `resume()` function, the test fails. Using the second mode of operation, we can perform a real Ajax testing using YUI Test, as shown in the following code snippet:

```
// Inside a test function
var this_local = this;

var successCallback = function(response) {
  this_local.resume(function() {
    // Assertions goes here to the response object...
  });
};
```

```
var failureCallback = function(response) {
  this_local.resume(function() {
    fail(); /* failure callback must not be called for successful
    scenario */
  });
};


asyncSystem.doAjaxOperation(inputData, successCallback,
failureCallback);


this.wait(5000); /* wait for 5 seconds until the resume is called
or timeout */
```

As shown in the preceding code snippet, two callbacks are created; one of
them represents the successful callback (successCallback) that is called
if the Ajax operation succeeds, and the other one represents the failure
callback (failureCallback) that is called if the Ajax operation fails. In both
successCallback and failureCallback, a call to the resume() API is done in
order to notify the wait() API that the server response is returned. The resume()
API has a single argument that represents a function that can have one or more
assertions. In successCallback, the argument function of the resume() API
can carry out assertions on the response parameter, which is returned from
the server response to verify that the server returns the correct results, while in
failureCallback, the argument function of the resume() API forces the test to
fail because it must not be called if the operation is completed successfully.

If the Ajax response is not returned from the server after five seconds (you can
set this to whatever duration you want), the wait() API will cause the test to fail.
Although this is a manual method, as opposed to Jasmine's waitsFor mechanism,
it is enough for real Ajax testing and will be used in order to test the Ajax part of the
weather application in the next section.

Testing the weather application

Now we come to developing the YUI tests for our weather application. Actually,
after you know how to write YUI tests for both synchronous and asynchronous
JavaScript (Ajax) code, testing the weather application is an easy task. As you
remember from the previous two chapters, we have three major JavaScript objects
in the weather application that we need to develop tests for—the LoginClient,
RegistrationClient, and WeatherClient objects.

Two subfolders, yuitest and tests , are created under the js-test folder (thus: yuitest\tests) to contain the YUI tests, as shown in the following screenshot:

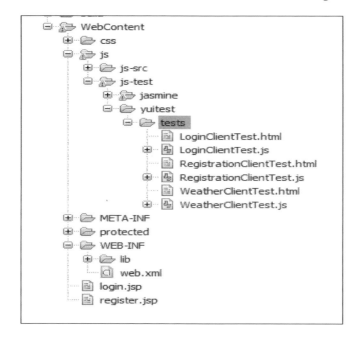

Because currently YUI Test does not have an API to load the HTML fixtures, they are included as part of the HTML test runner pages. As shown in the preceding screenshot, there are three HTML files that contain the HTML fixtures for every test—LoginClientTest.html, RegistrationClientTest.html, and WeatherClientTest.html. Every HTML file also includes the source and test JavaScript objects. There are three YUI test files (LoginClientTest.js, RegistrationClientTest.js, and WeatherClientTest.js) that test the main three JavaScript objects of the application.

Testing the LoginClient object

As what we did in *Chapter 2, Jasmine*, in the *Testing the LoginClient object* section we will perform unit testing for the following functionalities:

- Validation of empty username and password

- Validating that the username is in e-mail address format

- Validating that the password contains at least one digit, one capital and small letter, at least one special character, and six characters or more

In order to perform this test, two test cases are created; one for testing the validation of the empty fields (the username and password) and the other one for testing the validation of the fields' formats. The two test cases are grouped in a single test suite, `LoginClient Test Suite`. The following code snippet shows the validation of the empty fields' test case in the `LoginClientTest.js` file:

```
var emptyFieldsTestcase = new Y.Test.Case({
  name: "Empty userName and Password fields validation Testcase",

  setUp: function() {
    this.loginClient = new weatherapp.LoginClient();

    this.loginForm = {
      "userNameField" : "username",
      "passwordField" : "password",
      "userNameMessage" : "usernameMessage",
      "passwordMessage" : "passwordMessage"
    };
  },
  tearDown: function() {
    delete this.loginClient;
  delete this.loginForm;
  },
  testEmptyUserName: function() {
    document.getElementById("username").value = ""; /* setting
    username to empty */
    document.getElementById("password").value = "Admin@123";

    this.loginClient.validateLoginForm(this.loginForm);

    Y.Assert.areEqual("(field is required)",
    document.getElementById("usernameMessage").innerHTML);
  },
  testEmptyPassword: function() {
    document.getElementById("username").value =
    "someone@yahoo.com";
    document.getElementById("password").value = "";   /* setting
    password to empty */

    this.loginClient.validateLoginForm(this.loginForm);

    Y.Assert.areEqual("(field is required)",
    document.getElementById("passwordMessage").innerHTML);
    }
});
```

In the preceding code snippet, the `setUp` method creates an instance from `weatherapp.LoginClient` and creates the `loginForm` object, which holds the IDs of the HTML elements that are used in the test.

`testEmptyUserName` tests whether the `LoginClient` object is able to display an error message when the username is not entered. It sets an empty value in the `username` field and then calls the `validateLoginForm` API of the `LoginClient` object. Then it checks whether the `validateLoginForm` API produces the `"(field is required)"` message in the `usernameMessage` field by using the `Y.Assert.areEqual` assertion.

`testEmptyPassword` does the same thing, but with the `password` field, not with the `username` field.

The following code snippet shows the second test case, which validates the formats of the fields (username and password) in the `LoginClientTest.js` file:

```
var fieldsFormatTestcase = new Y.Test.Case({
  name: "Fields format validation Testcase",

  setUp: function() {
    this.loginClient = new weatherapp.LoginClient();

    this.loginForm = {
      "userNameField" : "username",
      "passwordField" : "password",
      "userNameMessage" : "usernameMessage",
      "passwordMessage" : "passwordMessage"
    };
  },
  tearDown: function() {
    delete this.loginClient;
    delete this.loginForm;
  },
  testUsernameFormat: function() {
    document.getElementById("username").value =
    "someone@someDomain";/* setting username to invalid format */
    document.getElementById("password").value = "Admin@123";

    this.loginClient.validateLoginForm(this.loginForm);

    Y.Assert.areEqual("(format is invalid)",
    document.getElementById("usernameMessage").innerHTML);
  },
  testPasswordFormat: function() {
    document.getElementById("username").value =
```

```
    "someone@someDomain.com";
    document.getElementById("password").value = "Admin123"; /*
    setting password to invalid format */

    this.loginClient.validateLoginForm(this.loginForm);

    Y.Assert.areEqual("(format is invalid)", document.getElementById("
passwordMessage").innerHTML);
    }
});
```

In the preceding code snippet, testUsernameFormat tests the validation of the username format. It tests whether the LoginClient object should be able to display an error message when the username format is not valid. It sets an invalid e-mail value in the username field and then calls the validateLoginForm API of the LoginClient object. Finally, it checks whether the validateLoginForm API produces the "(format is invalid)" message in the usernameMessage field by using the Y.Assert.areEqual assertion.

testPasswordFormat enters a password that does not comply with the application's password rules; it enters a password that does not include a capital letter and then calls the validateLoginForm API of the LoginClient object. It finally checks whether the validateLoginForm API produces the "(format is invalid)" message in the passwordMessage field.

emptyFieldsTestcase and fieldsFormatTestcase are added to the LoginClient test suite, the YUI console is created, the test suite is run, and the test results are displayed in the console component, as shown in the following code snippet from the LoginClientTest.js file:

```
var suite = new Y.Test.Suite("LoginClient Test Suite");

suite.add(emptyFieldsTestcase);
suite.add(fieldsFormatTestcase);

//create the console
var console = new Y.Console({
  style: 'block',
  newestOnTop : false
});
console.render('#resultsPanel');

Y.Test.Runner.add(suite);
Y.Test.Runner.run();
```

Finally, the following code snippet shows the HTML fixture of the `LoginClient` test suite in the `LoginClientTest.html` file. It includes the username and password fields, the YUI console `div` element, and both the source JavaScript object file (`LoginClient.js`) and the test JavaScript object file (`LoginClientTest.js`).

```
<label for="username">Username   <span id="usernameMessage"
class="error"></span></label>
<input type="text" id="username" name="username"/>
<label for="password">Password   <span id="passwordMessage"
class="error"></span></label>
<input type="password" id="password" name="password"/>

<div id="resultsPanel" class="yui3-skin-sam"></div>
...

<script type="text/javascript" src="../../../js-src/LoginClient.js"></
script>
<script type="text/javascript" src="LoginClientTest.js"></script>
```

Testing the RegistrationClient object

In the `RegistrationClient` object, we will verify the following functionalities:

- Validation of empty username and passwords
- Validation of matched passwords
- Validating that the username is in e-mail address format
- Validating that the password contains at least one digit, one capital and small letter, at least one special character, and six characters or more
- Validating that the user registration Ajax functionality is performed correctly

The first four functionalities will be skipped because they are pretty similar to the tests that are explained in the `LoginClient` test suite, so let's learn how to check whether the user registration (the `registerUser` test case) Ajax functionality is performed correctly.

The `registerUser` test case covers the following test scenarios:

- Testing the adding of a new user through the `testAddNewUser` test function. The registration client object should be able to register a valid user correctly.
- Testing the adding of a user with an existing user ID through the `testAddExistingUser` test function. In this case, the registration client object should fail when registering a user whose ID is already registered.

The following code snippet shows the `testAddNewUser` test function of the
`registerUser` test case in the `RegistrationClientTest.js` file. The `setUp`
method creates an instance from `weatherapp.RegistrationClient` and creates the
`registrationForm` object, which holds the IDs of the registration form that will be
used in the test.

```
var registerUserTestcase = new Y.Test.Case({
  name: "RegisterUser Testcase",

  setUp: function() {
    this.registrationClient = new weatherapp.RegistrationClient();

    this.registrationForm = {
        "userNameField" : "username",
        "passwordField1" : "password1",
        "passwordField2" : "password2",
        "userNameMessage" : "usernameMessage",
        "passwordMessage1" : "passwordMessage1"
    };
  },
  tearDown: function() {
    delete this.registrationClient;
    delete this.registrationForm;
  },
  testAddNewUser: function() {
    this.userName = "hazems" + new Date().getTime() +
    "@apache.org";

    document.getElementById("username").value = this.userName;
    document.getElementById("password1").value = "Admin@123";
    document.getElementById("password2").value = "Admin@123";

    var this_local = this;
    var Y_local = Y;

    var successCallback = function(response) {
      var resultMessage = response.xmlhttp.responseText;
      this_local.resume(function() {
        Y_local.Assert.areEqual("User is registered successfully
        ...", resultMessage);
      });
    };

    var failureCallback = function() {
```

```
        this_local.resume(function() {
          fail();
        });
      };

      this.registrationClient.registerUser(this.registrationForm,
      successCallback, failureCallback);

      this.wait(5000); /* wait for 5 seconds until the resume is
      called or timeout */
    }
    ...
  });
```

In the `testAddNewUser` test function, the registration form is filled with a valid generated username and valid matched passwords, and then two callbacks are created. The first callback is the success callback, while the second one is the failure callback. `registrationClient.registerUser` is called with the registration form, the success callback, and the failure callback parameters. `this.wait(5000)` waits for a call from the `resume()` API, or it fails after 5000 milliseconds.

In the success callback, the `resume()` API is called, and the `resume()` function parameter ensures that the returned response message from the server is `User is registered successfully` ... using the `areEqual` assertion.

In the failure callback, the `resume()` API is also called, and the `resume()` function parameter ensures that the test fails by using the `fail()` API because the failure callback must not be called for a valid user registration.

 The YUI Test Ajax testing of the weather application is *real* Ajax testing; this requires the server to be up and running in order to perform the test correctly.

The following code snippet shows the `testAddExistingUser` test function of the `registerUser` test case in the `RegistrationClientTest.js` file:

```
var registerUserTestcase = new Y.Test.Case({
  ...
    testAddExistingUser: function() {
    document.getElementById("username").value = this.userName;
    document.getElementById("password1").value = "Admin@123";
    document.getElementById("password2").value = "Admin@123";

    var this_local = this;
    var Y_local = Y;
```

```
      var successCallback = function() {
        this_local.resume(function() {
          fail();
        });
      };

      var failureCallback = function(response) {
        var resultMessage = response.xmlhttp.responseText;
        this_local.resume(function() {
          Y_local.Assert.areEqual("A user with the same username is
          already registered ...", resultMessage,);
        });
      };

      this.registrationClient.registerUser(this.registrationForm,
      successCallback, failureCallback);

      this.wait(5000); /* wait for 5 seconds until the resume is called
      or timeout */
    }
  });
```

In the `testAddExistingUser` test function, the registration form is filled with the same username that is already registered in the `testAddNewUser` test function, and then two callbacks are created. The first callback is the success callback while the second one is the failure callback. `registrationClient.registerUser` is called with the registration form, the success callback, and the failure callback parameters. The `this.wait(5000)` waits for a call to the `resume()` API or it fails after `5000` milliseconds.

In the success callback, the `resume()` API is called, and the `resume()` function parameter ensures that the test fails by using the `fail()` API because the success callback must not be called when registering a user whose ID is already registered.

In the failure callback, the `resume()` API is also called, and the `resume()` function parameter ensures that the returned failure response message from the server is A user with the same username is already registered ... using the `areEqual` assertion.

Finally, the following code snippet shows the HTML fixture of the
`RegistrationClient` test suite in the `RegistrationClientTest.html` file.
It includes the username and password fields, the YUI console `div` element, and both
the JavaScript source files, `RegistrationClient.js` and `LoginClient.js`, because
`RegistrationClient.js` depends on `LoginClient.js` and on the JavaScript test
file `RegistrationClientTest.js`.

```
...
<label for="username">Username (Email)  <span id="usernameMessage"
class="error"></span></label>
<input type="text" id="username" name="username"/><br/>

<label for="password1">Password  <span id="passwordMessage1"
class="error"></span></label>
<input type="password" id="password1" name="password1"/><br/>

<label for="password2">Confirm your password</label>
<input type="password" id="password2" name="password2"/><br/>

<div id="resultsPanel" class="yui3-skin-sam"></div>
...

<script type="text/javascript" src="../../../js-src/LoginClient.js"></
script>
<script type="text/javascript" src="../../../js-src/
RegistrationClient.js"></script>

<script type="text/javascript" src="RegistrationClientTest.js"></
script>
```

Testing the WeatherClient object

In the `WeatherClient` object, we will test the following functionalities:

- Getting the weather for a valid location
- Getting the weather for an invalid location (the system should display
  an error message for this case)

To test the `WeatherClient` object, the same technique that we used in the
`registerUser` test case is followed. Developing this test will be left for you as
an exercise. You can get the full source code for the `WeatherClientTest.js` and
`WeatherClientTest.html` files from the `Chapter 3` folder in the code bundle
available on the book's website.

To get the test source code, all that you need to do is to unzip the `weatherApplication.zip` file, and you will be able to find all the YUI tests in the `tests` folder in `weatherApplication\WebContent\js\js-test\yuitest`.

Running the weather application tests

In order to run the weather application tests correctly, you have to make sure that the server is up and running or the application will not pass the Ajax tests. So, you need to deploy this chapter's updated version of the weather application on Tomcat 6 as explained in *Chapter 1, Unit Testing JavaScript Applications,* and then type the three following URLs in the browser's address bar:

- `http://localhost:8080/weatherApplication/js/js-test/yuitest/ tests/LoginClientTest.html`

- `http://localhost:8080/weatherApplication/js/js-test/yuitest/ tests/RegistrationClientTest.html`

- `http://localhost:8080/weatherApplication/js/js-test/yuitest/ tests/WeatherClientTest.html`

 Don't worry; you do not need to do this every time you run the YUI Test pages. Check the *Integration with build management tools* section to learn how to automate the running of the YUI Test pages.

Generating test reports

In the *Integration with build management tools* section, YUI Test Selenium Driver is used to generate JUnit XML reports automatically without using the YUI Test reporting APIs. You may jump to that section if you are not interested in digging into the YUI Test reporting APIs.

YUI Test has a powerful feature, test reporting. Once the test completes its execution and the test result's object is retrieved, you can post the test results to the server (Java servlet, PHP, or another server-side object) to generate the report. First of all, let's see how to retrieve the test result's object.

In order to retrieve the test result's object, you need to use the `Y.Test.Runner. getResults()` API. Unfortunately, The `Y.Test.Runner.getResults()` API expects you to call it when the test is completed; in other words, it does not wait for the tests to complete its executions. If you call the `Y.Test.Runner.getResults()` API and the tests are still running, the API will return `null`.

However, to make sure that the test is completed, you have one of two options:

- The first is to use the `isRunning()` API in the `TestRunner` interface, which returns true if the test is still running and false if it finishes its execution. The following code snippet shows you how to call the `Y.Test.Runner.getResults()` API properly and ensure, using the `isRunning()` API, that it will not be called while the test is running:

```
var intervalID = window.setInterval(function() {
  if (! Y.Test.Runner.isRunning()) {
    var results = Y.Test.Runner.getResults();

    // Do whatever you want with the results

    window.clearInterval(intervalID);
  }
}, 1000);
```

  The code is simple; `window.setInterval` calls the `Y.Test.Runner.isRunning()` API every `1000` milliseconds and waits until `Y.Test.Runner.isRunning()` returns false. When `Y.Test.Runner.isRunning()` returns false, the `Y.Test.Runner.getResults()` API can be called safely, and then the execution of `window.setInterval` is stopped by calling `window.clearInterval(intervalID)`.

- The second option, which is the recommended one, is to subscribe in the YUI test runner complete event (`Y.Test.Runner.COMPLETE_EVENT`), as shown in the following code snippet:

```
function processTestResults() {
  var results = Y.Test.Runner.getResults();

  // Do whatever you want with the results
}

Y.Test.Runner.subscribe(Y.Test.Runner.COMPLETE_EVENT,
processTestResults);
```

  You can use the YUI test runner's `subscribe()` API in order to subscribe in the test runner's complete event. `processTestResults` is the event handler that is called once the event is completed. In the `processTestResults` event handler, it is safe to call the `Y.Test.Runner.getResults()` API to get the test results.

In YUI Test, there are many types of events that can be subscribed to. There are events on the level of the test, test case, test suite, and the test runner. The preceding code snippet is an example of an event on the test runner level. To get a complete reference for all the YUI Test events, check the following URL:

`http://yuilibrary.com/yui/docs/api/classes/Test.Runner.html#Events`

After getting the test results, let's learn how to post the results on the server to generate the report. The following code snippet shows how to send the test results data in JUnit XML format to the server. This code is part of the `RegistrationClientTest.js` file:

```
Y.Test.Runner.add(suite);

function processTestResults() {
  var results = Y.Test.Runner.getResults();
  var reporter = new
  Y.Test.Reporter("/weatherApplication/YUIReportViewer",
  Y.Test.Format.JUnitXML);

  // Some parameters to be sent

  reporter.report(results);
}

Y.Test.Runner.subscribe(Y.Test.Runner.COMPLETE_EVENT,
processTestResults);
Y.Test.Runner.run();
```

After getting the test result's object, you create a `Y.Test.Reporter` object, which can be constructed using the two following parameters:

- The server URL to post the test result's data to. Note that the POST data operation is performed silently by the `Y.Test.Reporter` object and does not cause the test page to navigate away because it does not get back any response from the server. In our example, the server URL is `/weatherApplication/YUIReportViewer`, which maps to a simple Java servlet that receives the posted test results data and saves the data in a file inside a local directory.

- The report format. The four following formats are allowed for the posting of test results:

  - ° `Y.Test.Format.XML`: To post the test results data in XML format.
  - ° `Y.Test.Format.JSON`: To post the test results data in JSON format.
  - ° `Y.Test.Format.JUnitXML`: To post the test results data in JUnit XML format.
  - ° `Y.Test.Format.TAP`: To post the test results in TAP format. TAP stands for **Test Anything Protocol**. For more information about this format, check the following URL:

    `http://testanything.org/wiki/index.php/Main_Page`

In order to post the test result data to the server, you need to call the `report()` API of the `Y.Test.Reporter` object with the test result data (`results`). By default, the following parameters are posted to the server when the `report()` API is called:

- `results`: The serialized test results data object
- `useragent`: The user-agent string that represents the browser
- `timestamp`: The date and time at which the report was sent

You have the ability to post extra parameters by using the `addField()` API, as shown in the following code snippet:

```
reporter.addField("param1", "value1");
reporter.addField("param2", "value2");
```

In order to make the report name and the report file extension configurable, the `addField()` API can be used in order to send this information to the `YUIReportViewer` custom servlet, as shown in the following code snippet:

```
Y.Test.Runner.add(suite);

function processTestResults() {
  var results = Y.Test.Runner.getResults();
  var reporter = new
  Y.Test.Reporter("/weatherApplication/YUIReportViewer",
  Y.Test.Format.JUnitXML);

  // Send a custom parameter to tell the Servlet the report
  name and extension.
  reporter.addField("reportName", "registrationTestReport");

  reporter.addField("format", "xml");
```

```
        reporter.report(results);
}


Y.Test.Runner.subscribe(Y.Test.Runner.COMPLETE_EVENT,
processTestResults);
Y.Test.Runner.run();
```

The custom `YUIReportViewer` servlet generates the report file with the `[reportName].[format]` name under the `yuitest\reports` folder. The report file contains the `results` content. The custom servlet code is included for your reference in the following code snippet; as you can see, it is very simple code that can be implemented easily in any other server-side technology such as PHP and ASP.NET.

```
public class YUIReportViewer extends HttpServlet {

   protected void doPost(HttpServletRequest request,
   HttpServletResponse response) throws ServletException,
   IOException {
     String results = request.getParameter("results");
     String format = (request.getParameter("format") == null) ?
     "xml" : request.getParameter("format");
     String reportName = (request.getParameter("reportName") ==
     null) ? "report" : request.getParameter("reportName");

   // Generate the report result file under the reports folder...
     BufferedWriter out = null;

     String reportFullPath =
     getServletContext().getRealPath("/js/js-test/yuitest/reports")
     + "/" + reportName + "." + format;

     try {
       FileWriter fstream = new FileWriter(reportFullPath);

       out = new BufferedWriter(fstream);
       out.write(results);
     } catch (Exception e) {
       e.printStackTrace();
     } finally {
       out.close();
     }
   }
}
```

> As indicated before, this book does not teach you any server-side technology (it is outside the scope of the book); however, it is good to mention the custom YUIReportViewer servlet code in this example in order to show you what the server-side code will look like in the case of generating a report.

After running the RegistrationClient test suite by browsing to http://localhost:8080/weatherApplication/js/js-test/yuitest/tests/RegistrationClientTest.html, the registrationTestReport.xml file can be accessed via http://localhost:8080/weatherApplication/js/js-test/yuitest/reports/registrationTestReport.xml. The following code snippet shows the RegistrationClient test report in JUnit XML format:

```
<testsuites>
  <testsuite name="Empty userName and Password fields Testcase"
  tests="2" failures="0" time="0.039">
    <testcase name="testEmptyUserName" time="0.003"/>
    <testcase name="testEmptyPassword" time="0.008"/>
  </testsuite>
  ...
  <testsuite name="RegisterUser Testcase" tests="2" failures="0"
  time="0.17">
    <testcase name="testAddNewUser" time="0.048"/>
    <testcase name="testAddExistingUser" time="0.062"/>
  </testsuite>
</testsuites>
```

You can produce a JSON report instead; change the format parameters of Y.Test.Reporter, as shown in the highlighted part of the following code snippet:

```
function processTestResults() {
  var results = Y.Test.Runner.getResults();
  var reporter = new
  Y.Test.Reporter("/weatherApplication/YUIReportViewer",
  Y.Test.Format.JSON);

  // Send a custom parameter to tell the Servlet the report
  name and extension.
  reporter.addField("reportName", "registrationTestReport");
  reporter.addField("format", "json");

  reporter.report(results);
}
```

After running the `RegistrationClient` **test suite,** `registrationTestReport.json` can be accessed via the following location:

```
http://localhost:8080/weatherApplication/js/js-test/yuitest/reports/
registrationTestReport.json
```

 You can follow the same procedure to generate YUI Test reports with different formats. All you need to do is to change the format parameter of the `Y.Test.Reporter` object, as shown in the previous examples.

Automation and integration with build management tools

It can be difficult to run every test page individually in order to check the results, so for example, if we have 100 YUI test pages, it means that we have to type 100 URLs in the browser's address bar, which is a very inefficient way of performing the tests. Fortunately, we can automate the running of the YUI test pages using **Selenium** (an automation web application testing tool) integration with YUI Test. This sort of integration can be done by the YUI Test Selenium Driver utility. Let's see how to work it.

Configuring YUI Test Selenium Driver

In order to configure the YUI Test Selenium Driver utility with the YUI tests, you need to do the following:

1. Make sure that you have installed Java 5 (v1.5 or later) on your operating system.

2. Download the following:

    ° The Selenium Server Version 2.25.0; it can be found at `http://seleniumhq.org/download/`.

    ° The Selenium Java Client Driver; it can be found at `https://github.com/yui/yuitest/blob/master/java/lib/selenium-java-client-driver.jar`.

    ° The YUI Test Selenium Driver, which can be found at `https://github.com/yui/yuitest/blob/master/java/build/yuitest-selenium-driver.jar.`.

3. Start the Selenium Server from the command line using `java -jar selenium-server-standalone-2.25.0.jar`.

4. Place the Selenium Java Client Driver (`selenium-java-client-driver.jar`) in `/lib/ext/`, in your JRE directory.

5. After following the preceding steps, YUI Test Selenium Driver (`yuitest-selenium-driver.jar`) is ready to execute the YUI tests.

Let's see how we will use the driver to automate the running of the weather application YUI tests.

Using YUI Test Selenium Driver in the weather application

YUI Test Selenium Driver works by communicating with the Selenium Server and specifying on which browsers the YUI test pages are to be loaded. The server then loads the test pages, and the JavaScript tests are executed in the specified browsers; once the tests are complete, the results are retrieved and then outputted into JUnit XML report files automatically (this is the default report format and it can be changed to XML or TAP formats from the driver configuration file).

In the weather application project, a `cli` folder is created under the `yuitest` folder to include the `yuitest-selenium-driver.jar` file and the command-line batch file that automates the running of the test pages (in case you are working in a Unix environment, you can create an equivalent `.sh` file). The following command shows how to automate running of the weather application test pages in the `runTests.bat` file (don't forget to make sure that Selenium Server is running before executing this command):

```
java -jar yuitest-selenium-driver.jar --browsers *firefox,*iexplore
--tests tests.xml --resultsdir %~dp0gen_reports
```

This command executes the `yuitest-selenium-driver.jar` file with the following parameters:

- `--browsers`: This parameter specifies which browsers will be used in the tests; in our case, Firefox and Internet Explorer are used.

- `--tests`: This parameter specifies the XML file that includes the YUI test pages. The content of this file is shown in the next code snippet.

- `--resultsdir`: This parameter specifies the location of the output report files. In our case, the output report files are generated in the `gen_reports` folder under the `cli` folder, which contains the batch file.

Let's see the content of the `tests.xml` file, which includes the weather application test pages, in the following code snippet:

```xml
<?xml version="1.0"?>
<yuitest>
    <tests base="http://localhost:8080/weatherApplication/js/js-test/
     yuitest/tests/" timeout="30000">
        <url>LoginClientTest.html</url>
        <url>RegistrationClientTest.html</url>
        <url>WeatherClientTest.html</url>
    </tests>
</yuitest>
```

The `tests.xml` file contains mainly three elements:

- The `<yuitest>` element, which represents the root element.

- The `<tests>` element, which includes the `<url>` tags of the different test pages. It has a `base` attribute that is used to specify the base location of all of the children `<url>` tags. In our case, this is `http://localhost:8080/weatherApplication/js/js-test/yuitest/tests/`. The `<tests>` element also has a `timeout` attribute that specifies the maximum number of milliseconds the driver will wait for the test to complete; after this period, an error will be thrown for the test. In our case, `30` seconds is specified.

- The `<url>` element, which contains the relative paths of the pages under the base URL specified in the `<tests>` parent element.

While running the command, you will find the application tests are executed in the Internet Explorer and Firefox browsers, as shown in the following screenshot:

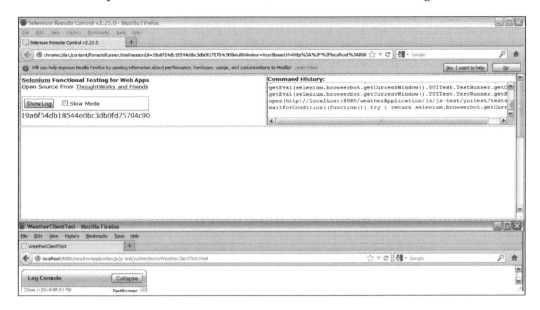

Once the tests are complete, the browsers will close automatically, and six JUnit XML test reports will be generated in the `gen_reports` folder—three reports for the three weather application test pages' execution results in Firefox and the other three reports for the execution results in IE.

Now you know how to use the driver in order to automate YUI tests. There are other parameters and features that are supported by the YUI Test Selenium Driver. You may check all of them in the driver documentation page in GitHub:

`https://github.com/yui/yuitest/wiki/Selenium-driver`

Integration with build management tools

Because the YUI Test Selenium Driver can run from the command line, it can be integrated easily with build management tools such as **Ant** and **Maven** and also with continuous integration tools such as **Hudson**. The following code snippet shows an Ant script (`ant.xml`) that runs the `runTests.bat` file:

```
<project name="weatherApplication" default="runYUITests" basedir=".">
  <target name="runYUITests">
    <exec executable="cmd">
```

```
      <arg value="/c"/>
      <arg value="runTests.bat"/>
    </exec>
  </target>
</project>
```

 For Hudson, you can create a **Hudson job** that periodically executes the `runTests.bat` file as a Windows batch command. Hudson is a continuous integration tool that provides an easy way for the software team to integrate the code changes to the software project. It allows the software team to produce up-to-date builds from the system easily through the automated continuous build (it can be done many times per day). More information about Hudson can be found at `http://hudson-ci.org/`.

Summary

In this chapter, you learned what YUI Test is and how to use the JavaScript unit testing framework to test synchronous JavaScript code. You also got to know how to test asynchronous (Ajax) JavaScript code by using the YUI Test `wait` and `resume` mechanism. You learned the various assertions provided by the framework, how to get the XML and JSON test reports using the framework reporter APIs, and how to generate the test reports automatically by using the YUI Test Selenium Driver. You also learned how to automate the YUI tests using the YUI Test Selenium Driver and how to integrate the automation script with Ant as an example of the build management tools. Along the way, we applied all of these concepts to test our weather application. In the next chapter, you will learn how to work with the QUnit framework and how to use it to test the weather application.

4
QUnit

QUnit is a popular JavaScript unit testing framework. Although QUnit is used and maintained by jQuery, it can be used for testing any independent JavaScript code. QUnit provides a simple syntax for creating JavaScript test modules and functions that can be run from the browser. QUnit provides a clean mechanism for testing asynchronous (Ajax) JavaScript code. In this chapter, the QUnit framework will be illustrated in detail and used for testing the weather application that was discussed in *Chapter 1, Unit Testing JavaScript Applications*.

Configuration

In order to configure QUnit, the first step is to download the two framework files:

- The **QUnit JS** file found at `http://code.jquery.com/qunit/qunit-1.10.0.js`
- The **QUnit CSS** file found at `http://code.jquery.com/qunit/qunit-1.10.0.css`

After downloading the two files, put them in the same folder. (Let's call this folder `lib`.) At the time of this writing, the latest release of QUnit is the v1.10.0, which will be used in this book.

Now, let's prepare the tests' runner page of the QUnit test runner page. The following code snippet shows the `BasicRunner.html` page that contains the basic skeleton of the QUnit test runner page:

```
<!DOCTYPE html>
<html>
<head>
  <meta charset="utf-8">
  <title>QUnit test runner</title>
  <link rel="stylesheet" href="lib/qunit-1.10.0.css">
```

```
    </head>
    <body>
      <div id="qunit"></div>
      <div id="qunit-fixture"></div>
      <script src="lib/qunit-1.10.0.js"></script>

      ...The test code here...
    </body>
    </html>
```

The BasicRunner.html page includes the framework files from the lib folder. As you will notice, there are two div elements in the test runner page. The first qunit div element is used for displaying the QUnit test results while the second qunit-fixture div element is used for holding the QUnit HTML fixtures needed for the tests.

 QUnit cleans up the qunit-fixture div element before every test run so you do not have to do this clean up manually.

Now you can run the test runner page that does not include any of the QUnit tests yet. The following screenshot shows the BasicRunner.html page, which does not include any tests:

Writing your first QUnit test

A QUnit test can contain test modules and test functions. A QUnit test module is a group of related test functions. Every test function should contain one or more assertion(s) in order to perform the test and verify the outputs.

The QUnit module function is responsible for creating the QUnit module and the QUnit test function is responsible for creating the QUnit test. In order to add the test function to the module, just place the test function under the declared module, as shown in the following code snippet:

```
module("testing Module", {
  setup: function() {
    // setup code goes here...
  }, teardown: function() {
    // teardown code goes here...
  }
});

test("testing function1", function() {
  // assertions go here...
});

test("testing function2", function() {
  // assertions go here...
});
```

As shown in the preceding code snippet, a test module with the name `"testing Module"` is created. The test module can contain a `setup` method that is called to perform the initialization of every test function before its execution. The test module can also contain a `teardown` method that is called after the execution of every test function, for de-initializing the test. The test module contains two test functions. The first test function is named `"testing function1"` while the second test function is named `"testing function2"`. Every test function can contain one or more assertions.

 In QUnit, you have the option to create the test functions without including them in modules. However, it is preferred to include tests in modules to organize them. Grouping the tests in modules gives you the ability to run every module independently.

Let's move to testing the `SimpleMath` JavaScript object (which we tested using the Jasmine and YUI Test frameworks in the previous chapters). The following code snippet reminds you with the code of the `SimpleMath` object:

```
SimpleMath = function() {
};

SimpleMath.prototype.getFactorial = function (number) {

  if (number < 0) {
    throw new Error("There is no factorial for negative numbers");
  }
  else if (number == 1 || number == 0) {

    // If number <= 1 then number! = 1.
```

```
            return 1;
        } else {

            // If number > 1 then number! = number * (number-1)!
            return number * this.getFactorial(number-1);
        }
    }

    SimpleMath.prototype.signum = function (number) {
        if (number > 0)  {
        return 1;
        } else if (number == 0) {
        return 0;
        } else {
        return -1;
        }
    }


    SimpleMath.prototype.average = function (number1, number2) {
        return (number1 + number2) / 2;
    }
```

In order to organize the `SimpleMath` QUnit tests, three modules are created for testing the `getFactorial`, `signum`, and `average` APIs of the `SimpleMath` object.

As we did in the previous chapters, we will develop the following three test scenarios for the `getFactorial` method:

- Positive number
- Zero
- Negative number

The following code snippet shows how to test the `getFactorial` module calculating the factorial of a positive number (3), 0, and a negative number (-10), using QUnit:

```
module("Factorial", {
  setup: function() {
    this.simpleMath = new SimpleMath();
  }, teardown: function() {
    delete this.simpleMath;
  }
});

test("calculating factorial for a positive number", function() {
  equal(this.simpleMath.getFactorial(3), 6, "Factorial of three
```

```
   must equal six");
});


test("calculating factorial for zero", function() {
  equal(this.simpleMath.getFactorial(0), 1, "Factorial of zero
  must equal one");
});


test("throwing an error when calculating the factorial for a negative
number", function() {
  raises(function() {
      this.simpleMath.getFactorial(-10)
    }, "There is no factorial for negative numbers");
});
```

The `module` function declares a new module called `Factorial`. In the `setup` method, the `simpleMath` object is created using `new SimpleMath()`. `tearDown` is used to clean up by deleting the created `simpleMath` object.

In the first test function of the `Factorial` module, the QUnit `equal` assertion function calls `simpleMath.getFactorial(3)` and expects the result to be equal to 6. If `simpleMath.getFactorial(3)` returns a value other than 6, then the test function fails. The last parameter of the QUnit `equal` assertion is an optional one, and it represents the message to be displayed with the test.

In the second test function of the `Factorial` module, the `equal` assertion function calls `simpleMath.getFactorial(0)` and expects it to be equal to 1. In the last test function of the `Factorial` module, the test function calls `simpleMath.getFactorial(-10)` and expects it to throw an error using the `raises` assertion.

The `raises` assertion takes two parameters; the first one is the `function` parameter that includes the call to the API to test, and the second one is an optional one and represents the message that is to be displayed with the test. The `raises` assertion succeeds if the API that is to be tested throws an error.

QUnit has other assertions to use instead of the `equal` and `raises` assertions; we will discuss them in more detail later in this chapter in the *Assertions* section.

After finalizing the `Factorial` module, we come to the new module that tests the functionality of the `signum` API provided by the `SimpleMath` object. The following code snippet shows the `Signum` module:

```
module("Signum", {
  setup: function() {
    this.simpleMath = new SimpleMath();
  }, teardown: function() {
```

```
    delete this.simpleMath;
  }
});

test("calculating signum for a positive number", function() {
  equal(this.simpleMath.signum(3), 1, "Signum of three must equal
  one");
});

test("calculating signum for zero", function() {
  equal(this.simpleMath.signum(0), 0, "Signum of zero must equal
  zero");
});

test("calculating signum for a negative number", function() {
  equal(this.simpleMath.signum(-1000), -1, "Signum of -1000 must
  equal -1");
});
```

We have three test functions in the `Signum` module; the first test function tests the signum of a positive number, the second test function tests the signum of zero, and the last test function tests the signum of a negative number. The following code snippet shows the `Average` module:

```
module("Average", {
  setup: function() {
    this.simpleMath = new SimpleMath();
  }, teardown: function() {
    delete this.simpleMath;
  }
});

test("calculating the average of two numbers", function() {
  equal(this.simpleMath.average(3, 6), 4.5, "Average of 3 and 6 must
equal 4.5");
});
```

In the `Average` module, the `"calculating the average of two numbers"` test function ensures that the average is calculated correctly by calling the `average` API using the two parameters 3 and 6, and expecting the result to be 4.5 using the `equal` assertion.

A very important thing that you should know is that QUnit does not guarantee the order of executing the test functions, so you must make every test function atomic; that is, every test function must not depend on any other test functions. For example, do not do the following in QUnit:

```
var counter = 0;
test("test function1", function() {
  counter++;
  equal(counter, 1, "counter should be 1");
});
test("test function2", function() {
  counter += 20;
  equal(counter, 21, "counter should be 21");
});
test("test function3", function() {
  counter += 10;
  equal(counter, 31, "counter should be 31");
});
```

In order to run the SimpleMath QUnit tests, we need to include the SimpleMath.js and simpleMathTest.js (which contains the unit tests of the SimpleMath object) files in the test runner page, as shown in the following code snippet:

```
<!DOCTYPE html>
<html>
<head>
  <meta charset="utf-8">
  <title>QUnit test runner</title>
  <link rel="stylesheet" href="lib/qunit-1.10.0.css">
</head>
<body>
  <div id="qunit"></div>
  <div id="qunit-fixture"></div>
  <script src="lib/qunit-1.10.0.js"></script>

  <script src="src/simpleMath.js"></script>
  <script src="tests/simpleMathTest.js"></script>
</body>
</html>
```

After clicking the `SimpleMath` QUnit test page `testRunner.html`, you will find the test results as shown in the following screenshot:

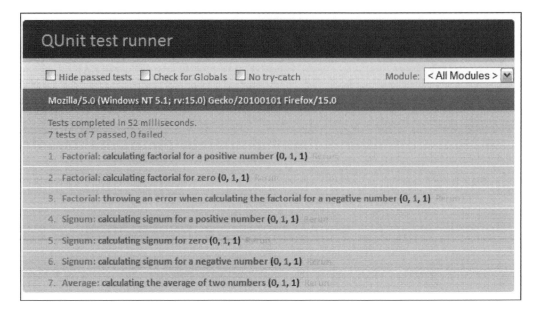

Assertions

An assertion is a function that validates a condition if the condition is not valid; it throws an error that causes the test function to fail. A test function can include one or more assertions; all the assertions have to pass in order to have the test function pass. In the first QUnit test example, we used the QUnit `equal` and `raises` assertions. In this section, the most important QUnit built-in assertions will be illustrated in more detail.

The ok assertion

The `ok` assertion takes two parameters. The first parameter is a condition and the second parameter is optional and represents the message that is to be displayed with the test. The `ok` assertion is passed if the condition is true. For example, the following examples will pass:

```
ok(true, "true passes");
ok(4==4, "4 must equal 4");
ok("some string", "Non-empty string passes");
```

The equal and notEqual assertions

The `equal` assertion has three parameters; the first two parameters represent the actual and expected values, and the third parameter is optional and represents the message that is to be displayed with the test. The `equal` assertion is passed if the actual parameter is equal to the expected parameter. The `notEqual` assertion ensures that the actual and expected parameters are not equal.

It is very important to know that the `equal` and `notEqual` assertions use the JavaScript `==` operator in order to perform the comparison, that is, they make the comparison and neglect the types. For example, the following assertions will pass:

```
equal(5, 5, "5 should equal 5...");
equal(5, "5", "5 should equal '5'...");
notEqual(5, 6, "5 should not equal 6...");
notEqual(5, "6", "5 should not equal '6'...");
```

The deepEqual and notDeepEqual assertions

The `deepEqual` assertion is more powerful than the `equal` assertion. It makes a deep comparison (recursively) between objects, arrays, and primitive datatypes. Unlike the `equal` assertion, the `deepEqual` assertion uses the `===` operator to perform the comparison (that is, it does not ignore the types). The `notDeepEqual` assertion function does the reverse operation of the `deepEqual` assertion. For example, the following assertions will pass:

```
// Objects comparison
var object1 = {a:1, b:2, c : {c1: 11, c2: 12}};
var object2 = {a:1, b:2, c : {c1: 11, c2: 12}};
var object3 = {a:1, b:"2", c : {c1: 11, c2: 12}};
deepEqual(object1, object2, "object1 should equal object2");
notDeepEqual(object1, object3, "object1 should not equal object3");

// Primitive comparison
deepEqual(1, 1, "1 === 1");
notDeepEqual(1, "1", "1 !== '1'");
```

As you will notice in the preceding code snippet, `object3` does not equal `object1` because the `deepEqual` assertion uses the `===` operator; this means that `b:2` does not equal `b:"2"`.

The expect assertion

The `expect` assertion is used for defining the number of assertions that the test function must contain. If the test function is completed without the correct number of assertions specified in the `expect` parameter, the test fails. For example, the following test function will fail:

```
test("test function1", function() {
  expect(3);
  ok(true);
  equal(1, 1);
});
```

The test fails because the `expect(3)` expects to see three assertions in the test function. If we insert the third assertion, the test function passes, as follows:

```
test("test function1", function() {
  expect(3);
  ok(true);
  equal(1, 1);
  deepEqual("1", "1");
});
```

Instead of using the `expect` assertion, the expectation count can be passed as the second parameter to the `test` function, as follows:

```
test("test function1", 3, function() {
  ok(true);
  equal(1, 1);
  deepEqual("1", "1");
});
```

> The `expect` assertion can be useful when you have a probability of *not* executing one or more assertions in your QUnit test code due to some reason, such as an operation failure. This can happen while testing asynchronous operations for which the execution of one or more assertions cannot be guaranteed if the operation fails or times out. The only remaining important, built-in assertion is the `raises` assertion, and you already know how it works in the `SimpleMath` object example.

Developing custom QUnit assertions

Adding to the mentioned built-in QUnit assertions, QUnit enables you to develop custom assertions to have more powerful and descriptive testing code. Let's develop two custom assertions, which are the `isPrimeNumber` and `sum` assertions, in order to understand how to develop custom assertions in QUnit.

The purpose of the `isPrimeNumber(number, message)` assertion is to check if the passed number is a prime number, while the `sum(number1, number2, result, message)` assertion checks if the sum of its first two number arguments is equal to the third number argument.

In order to define a custom assertion in QUnit, you should use the `QUnit.push` API. The `QUnit.push` API has the following parameters:

- `result`: If it is set to true, this means that the test succeeds, and if it is set to false, this means that the test fails

- `actual`: It represents the actual value

- `expected`: It represents the expected value

- `message`: It represents the message that is to be displayed with the test function

The main usage of the `actual` and `expected` parameters is that they are used by the QUnit framework in order to help the developer troubleshoot the test when it fails, as shown in the next screenshot. Let's start implementing the `sum` custom assertion. The following code snippet shows the `sum` custom assertion code:

```
function sum(number1, number2, result, message) {
  var expected = number1 + " + " + number2 + " = " + result;
  var actual = expected;

  if ((number1 + number2) != result) {
    actual = number1 + " + " + number2 + " != " + result;
  }

  QUnit.push((number1 + number2) == result, actual, expected,
  message);
}
```

The first parameter of the `QUnit.push` API is set to the Boolean result for checking that the summation of `number1` and `number2` is equal to `result`. When the two numbers `number1` and `number2` are not equal to `result`, the `actual` and `expected` parameters should have meaningful values in order to help the developer debug the failing test. The `actual` parameter is set to `number1 + number2 != result` while the `expected` parameter is always set to `number1 + number2 = result`.

The `sum` custom assertion, works just like any other QUnit assertion. You can use it as in the following code snippet:

```
sum(30, 20, 50, "50 = 30 + 20");
```

The next test will fail and the result will be displayed, as shown in the following screenshot:

```
sum(30, 20, 55, "55 != 30 + 20");
```

As shown in the previous screenshot, when the test fails, QUnit uses the `actual` and `expected` parameters that are set in the custom assertion to display the **Expected**, **Result**, and **Diff** items for helping the developer debug the test. The following code snippet shows the `isPrimeNumber` custom assertion code:

```
function isPrimeNumber(number, message) {
    if (number < 2) {
        QUnit.push(false, false, true, message);
        return;
    }

    var n = Math.sqrt(number);

    for (var i = 2; i <= n; ++i) {
        if (number % i == 0) {
            QUnit.push(false, false, true, message);
            return;
        }
    }
}
```

```
   QUnit.push(true, true, true, message);
   return;
}
```

If the passed `number` parameter is not a prime number, then the first parameter of the `QUnit.push` API is set to `false` in order to fail the test. The `actual` parameter is set to `false` while the `expected` parameter is set to `true` in order to show the error details in the test runner page. The following code snippet shows the complete code and usage of the custom assertions:

```
function sum(number1, number2, result, message) {
  var expected = number1 + " + " + number2 + " = " + result;
  var actual = expected;

  if ((number1 + number2) != result) {
    actual = number1 + " + " + number2 + " != " + result;
  }

  QUnit.push((number1 + number2) == result, actual, expected,
  message);
}

function isPrimeNumber(number, message) {
  if (number < 2) {
    QUnit.push(false, false, true, message);
    return;
  }

  var n = Math.sqrt(number);

  for (var i = 2; i <= n; ++i) {
    if (number % i == 0) {
      QUnit.push(false, false, true, message);
      return;
    }
  }

  QUnit.push(true, true, true, message);
  return;
}

test("custom assertion test", function() {
  sum(30, 20, 50, "50 = 30 + 20");
  isPrimeNumber(23, "23 is prime");
});
```

After running the preceding code snippet, the QUnit test runner page will display the successful test results of the custom assertions, as shown in the following screenshot:

Testing asynchronous (Ajax) JavaScript code

The common question that comes to mind is how to test asynchronous (Ajax) JavaScript code using QUnit. What has been mentioned in the chapter so far is how to perform unit testing for synchronous JavaScript code. QUnit provides two main APIs, namely stop() and start(), in order to perform real Ajax testing. Let me show you how to use them.

The stop and start APIs

The stop() API stops the QUnit test runner until the start() API is called or the test function is timed out. For example:

```
QUnit.config.testTimeout = 10000;
test("test function1", function() {
  stop();

  window.setTimeout(function() {
    ok(true);
    start();
  }, 3000);
});
```

As shown in the preceding code snippet, the `"test function1"` function stops the QUnit test runner by calling the `stop()` API. The `window.setTimeout` function resumes the test runner by calling the `start()` API after `3000` milliseconds.

In order to specify the test function timeout, you can set the global property `QUnit.config.testTimeout` to the time in milliseconds. In the previous example, it is set to `10000` milliseconds (10 seconds).

QUnit has another way of working with asynchronous operations; instead of explicitly calling the `stop()` API in the test method, you can directly use the `asyncTest` function as follows:

```
asyncTest("test function1", function() {
  window.setTimeout(function() {
    ok(true);
    start();
  }, 3000);
});
```

Using one of the two mentioned approaches, you can perform real Ajax testing. The following code snippet shows you how to create a real Ajax test using the `asyncTest` function:

```
QUnit.config.testTimeout = 10000;
asyncTest("Making a REAL Ajax testing", function() {
  var successCallback = function(response) {
    var resultMessage = response.xmlhttp.responseText;

    // Validate the result message using the QUnit assertions.

    start();
  };

  var failureCallback = function() {
    ok(false, "MUST fail");
    start();
  };

  asyncSystem.doAjaxOperation(inputData, successCallback,
  failureCallback);
});
```

As shown in the previous code snippet, two callbacks are created; one of them represents the successful callback (successCallback) that is called if the Ajax operation succeeds, and the other one represents the failure callback (failureCallback) that is called if the Ajax operation fails. In both successCallback and failureCallback, a call to the start() API is made in order to notify the QUnit asynchronous test that the server response is returned and the test runner can resume. In successCallback, there should be calls to the QUnit assertions in order to validate the returned Ajax response, and in failureCallback, the ok(false) expression forces the test to fail because the failure callback should not be called if the asynchronous operation succeeds.

If the Ajax response is not returned from the server after 10 seconds (you can set it to whatever duration you want using QUnit.config.testTimeout), the test will fail. In the *Testing the weather application* section, the two provided QUnit Ajax testing approaches will be used in order to test the Ajax part of the weather application.

Testing the weather application

Now, we come to developing the QUnit tests for our weather application. Actually, after you have learned how to write QUnit tests for both synchronous and asynchronous JavaScript (Ajax) code, testing the weather application is an easy task. As you remember from the previous chapters, we have three major JavaScript objects in the weather application that we need for developing tests for the LoginClient, RegistrationClient, and WeatherClient objects.

Two subfolders qunit and tests are created under the js-test folder (thus: qunit\tests) for containing the QUnit tests, and the lib folder is created under the qunit folder (thus: qunit\lib) for containing QUnit library files, as shown in the following screenshot:

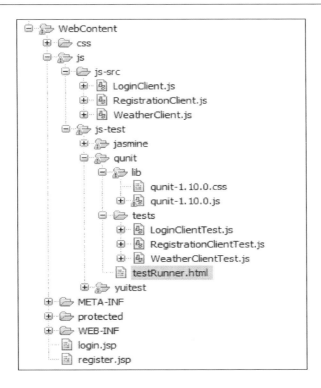

The tests folder contains three main JavaScript files (LoginClientTest.js, RegistartionClientTest.js, and WeatherClientTest.js) for testing the weather application's corresponding JavaScript objects. The QUnit test runner file testRunner.html is placed directly under the qunit folder in the js-test folder (thus: js-test\qunit). The following code snippet shows the contents of the QUnit testRunner.html page of the weather application:

```
<!DOCTYPE html>
<html>
<head>
  <meta charset="utf-8">
  <title>QUnit test runner</title>
  <link rel="stylesheet" href="lib/qunit-1.10.0.css">
</head>
<body>
  <div id="qunit"></div>
  <div id="qunit-fixture"></div>
  <script src="lib/qunit-1.10.0.js"></script>

  <!-- Source files -->
  <script type="text/javascript" src="../../js-
```

```
src/LoginClient.js"></script>
<script type="text/javascript" src="../../js-
src/RegistrationClient.js"></script>
<script type="text/javascript" src="../../js-
src/WeatherClient.js"></script>

<!-- Test files -->
<script src="tests/LoginClientTest.js"></script>
<script src="tests/RegistrationClientTest.js"></script>
<script src="tests/WeatherClientTest.js"></script>

</body>
</html>
```

As shown in the `testRunner.html` page, both the source and test JavaScript files are included in the page. In each of the test files, a QUnit module that will be responsible for testing the corresponding JavaScript object will be created.

Testing the LoginClient object

As we did in the previous chapters, in the *Testing the LoginClient object* section we will perform unit testing for the following functionalities:

- Validation of empty username and password

- Validating that the username is in e-mail address format

- Validating that the password contains at least one digit, one capital and small character, at least one special character, and six characters or more

In order to perform this test, a module `"LoginClient Test Module"` that groups all of these tests is created. The following code snippet shows the definition of `"LoginClient Test Module"`:

```
module("LoginClient Test Module", {
  setup: function() {

    // The HTML fixture for the LoginClient.
    document.getElementById("qunit-fixture").innerHTML =
      "<label for=\"username\">Username  <span
      id=\"usernameMessage\"></span></label>" +
       "<input type=\"text\" id=\"username\" name=\"username\"/>"
       +
       "<label for=\"password\">Password  <span
       id=\"passwordMessage\"></span></label>" +
       "<input type=\"password\" id=\"password\"
       name=\"password\"/>";
```

```
        this.loginClient = new weatherapp.LoginClient();

        this.loginForm = {
            "userNameField" : "username",
            "passwordField" : "password",
            "userNameMessage" : "usernameMessage",
            "passwordMessage" : "passwordMessage"
        };
    }, teardown: function() {
      delete this.loginClient;
      delete this.loginForm;
    }
});
```

The setup method of "LoginClient Test Module" appends the HTML fixture that is needed by the LoginClient test to the qunit-fixture div (the HTML fixture contains the username and password input fields and labels), and then creates an instance from weatherapp.LoginClient and creates the loginForm object, which holds the IDs of the HTML elements that are used in the test.

The following code snippet shows the empty username and password test functions of "LoginClient Test Module":

```
test("validating empty username", function() {
  document.getElementById("username").value = ""; /* setting
  username to empty */
  document.getElementById("password").value = "Admin@123";

  this.loginClient.validateLoginForm(this.loginForm);

  equal(document.getElementById("usernameMessage").innerHTML,
  "(field is required)", "validating empty username ...");
});

test("validating empty password", function() {
  document.getElementById("username").value = "someone@yahoo.com";
  document.getElementById("password").value = "";    /* setting
  password to empty */

  this.loginClient.validateLoginForm(this.loginForm);

  equal(document.getElementById("passwordMessage").innerHTML,
  "(field is required)", "validating empty password ...");
});
```

The "validating empty username" test function tests LoginClient to ensure that it is able to display an error message when the username is not entered. It sets an empty value in the username field and then calls the validateLoginForm API of the LoginClient object; then it verifies that the validateLoginForm API produces the "(field is required)" message in the usernameMessage field using the equal assertion.

The "validating empty password" test function does the same thing but with the password field and not with the username field.

The following code snippet shows the test functions of the "LoginClient Test Module", which validate the formats of the fields (the username and the password):

```
test("validating username format", function() {
    document.getElementById("username").value = "someone@yahoo"; /*
    setting username to incorrect format */
    document.getElementById("password").value = "Admin@123";

    this.loginClient.validateLoginForm(this.loginForm);

    equal(document.getElementById("usernameMessage").innerHTML,
    "(format is invalid)", "validating username format ...");
});

test("validating password format", function() {
  document.getElementById("username").value = "someone@yahoo.com";
  document.getElementById("password").value = "admin@123";   /*
  setting password to incorrect format */

  this.loginClient.validateLoginForm(this.loginForm);

  equal(document.getElementById("passwordMessage").innerHTML,
  "(format is invalid)", "validating password format ...");
});
```

The "validating username format" test function tests the validation of the username format. It tests the LoginClient object to ensure that it is able to display an error message when the username format is not valid. It sets an invalid e-mail value in the username field and then calls the validateLoginForm API of LoginClient. Finally, it checks that the validateLoginForm API produces the "(format is invalid)" message in the usernameMessage field, using the equal assertion.

The `"validating password format"` function enters a password that does not comply with the application's password rules; it enters a password that does not include a capital letter and then calls the `validateLoginForm` API of `LoginClient`. It finally checks that the `validateLoginForm` API produces the `"(format is invalid)"` message in the `passwordMessage` field.

Testing the RegistrationClient object

In the `RegistrationClient` object, we will test the following functionalities:

- Validation of empty username and passwords
- Validation of matched passwords
- Validating that the username is in e-mail address format
- Validating that the password contains at least one digit, one capital and small character, at least one special character, and six characters or more
- Validating that the user registration Ajax functionality is performed correctly

Testing of the first four functionalities will be skipped because they are pretty similar to the tests that are explained in `"LoginClient Test Module"`, so let's see how to verify that the user registration (`registerUser`) Ajax functionality is performed correctly.

The `registerUser` tests cover the following test scenarios:

- Testing adding a new user with a unique user ID.
- Testing adding a user with an existing user ID. In this case, the registration client should fail when registering a user whose ID is already registered.

`"RegistrationClient Test Module"` groups all the `RegistrationClient` tests. The following code snippet shows the definition of the `"RegistrationClient Test Module"`:

```
module("RegistrationClient Test Module", {
  setup: function() {

    // The HTML fixture for the RegistrationClient.
    document.getElementById("qunit-fixture").innerHTML =
      "<label for=\"username\">Username (Email)  <span
      id=\"usernameMessage\"></span></label>" +
      "<input type=\"text\" id=\"username\" name=\"username\"/>" +
      "<label for=\"password1\">Password  <span
      id=\"passwordMessage1\"></span></label>" +
      "<input type=\"password\" id=\"password1\"
```

```
            name=\"password1\"/>" +
            "<label for=\"password2\">Confirm your password</label>" +
            "<input type=\"password\" id=\"password2\"
            name=\"password2\"/>";

        this.registrationClient = new weatherapp.RegistrationClient();

        this.registrationForm = {
            "userNameField" : "username",
            "passwordField1" : "password1",
            "passwordField2" : "password2",
            "userNameMessage" : "usernameMessage",
            "passwordMessage1" : "passwordMessage1"
        };
    }, teardown: function() {
      delete this.registrationClient;
      delete this.registrationForm;
    }
});
```

The setup method of "RegistrationClient Test Module" appends the HTML fixture of the RegistrationClient test to the qunit-fixture div (the HTML fixture contains the username and passwords input fields and labels), and then creates an instance from weatherapp.RegistrationClient and creates the registrationForm object, which holds the IDs of the HTML elements that are used in the test. The following code snippet shows the first part of the "testing the registration feature" test function of "RegistrationClient Test Module", which tests registering a new user using the registerUser API:

```
QUnit.config.testTimeout = 10000;
test("testing the registration feature", function() {

    // Register a new user with a unique user name.
    stop();

    this.userName = "hazems" + new Date().getTime() + "@apache.org";

    document.getElementById("username").value = this.userName;
    document.getElementById("password1").value = "Admin@123";
    document.getElementById("password2").value = "Admin@123";
    var local_this = this;
```

```
var newSuccessCallback = function(response) {
  var resultMessage = response.xmlhttp.responseText;
  equal(resultMessage, "User is registered successfully ...",
  "Registering a new user succeeded ...");
  start();

  // Register the created user again to check that the
    registration will fail.
    // The code will be shown in the next code snippet ...

};

var newFailureCallback = function() {
  ok(false, "Registering a new user failed ...");
  start();
};

this.registrationClient.registerUser(this.registrationForm,
newSuccessCallback, newFailureCallback);
});
```

In the test function, the `stop()` API waits for a call from the `start()` API, or it fails the test function after `10000` milliseconds. The registration form is filled with a valid generated username and valid matched passwords, and then two callbacks are created. The first callback represents the success callback while the second one represents the failure callback. `registrationClient.registerUser` is called with the registration form, the success callback, and the failure callback parameters.

In the success callback, the response message returned from the server is ensured of being equal to the `"User is registered successfully ..."` message using the `equal` assertion, and then a call is made to the `start()` API to proceed with the test.

In the failure callback, the `ok(false)` is called in order to fail the test function, because the failure callback should not be called if the registration is performed successfully, and then a call is made to the `start()` API to proceed with the test.

The QUnit Ajax testing of the weather application is *real* Ajax testing; this requires the server to be up and running in order to perform the test correctly.

The following code snippet shows the second part of the "testing the registration feature" test function that was not shown in the preceding code. The second part contains the second test scenario of the registerUser API that tests registering the created user again in order to ensure that the registerUser API will fail (because the username already exists):

```
stop();

var existingSuccessCallback = function(response) {
    ok(false, "Validating registering a user with an existing id
    failed ...");
    start();
};

var existingFailureCallback = function(response) {
    var resultMessage = response.xmlhttp.responseText;
    equal(resultMessage, "A user with the same username is already
    registered ...", "Validating registering a user with an existing
    id succeeded ...");
    start();
};

local_this.registrationClient.registerUser(local_this.
registrationForm, existingSuccessCallback, existingFailureCallback);
```

The stop() API waits for a call to the start() API, or it fails after the timeout period has passed. The registration form is still holding the same username that has already been registered in the first test scenario of the test function, and two callbacks are created. The first callback (existingSuccessCallback) represents the success callback while the second one (existingFailureCallback) represents the failure callback. registrationClient.registerUser is called with the registration form, the success callback, and the failure callback parameters.

In the success callback, ok(false) is called in order to fail the test function because the success callback must not be called in this case, and then a call is made to the start() API to proceed with the test. In the failure callback, the returned response message from the server is ensured to equal the "A user with the same username is already registered ..." message using the equal assertion, and then a call is made to the start() API to proceed with the test.

The following code snippet shows the complete code of the "testing the registration feature" function of "RegistrationClient Test Module":

```
QUnit.config.testTimeout = 10000;
test("testing the registration feature", function() {

    // Register a new user.
    stop();
```

```
this.userName = "hazems" + new Date().getTime() + "@apache.org";

document.getElementById("username").value = this.userName;
document.getElementById("password1").value = "Admin@123";
document.getElementById("password2").value = "Admin@123";

var local_this = this;

var newSuccessCallback = function(response) {
  var resultMessage = response.xmlhttp.responseText;
  equal(resultMessage, "User is registered successfully ...",
  "Registering a new user succeeded ...");
  start();

  // Register the created user again (Register an existing
     user).
  stop();

  var existingSuccessCallback = function(response) {
    ok(false, "Validating registering a user with an existing id
    failed ...");
    start();
  };

  var existingFailureCallback = function(response) {
    var resultMessage = response.xmlhttp.responseText;
    equal(resultMessage, "A user with the same username is
    already registered ...", "Validating registering a user with
    an existing id succeeded ...");
    start();
  };

  local_this.registrationClient.registerUser(local_this.
registrationForm, existingSuccessCallback, existingFailureCallback);
  };

  var newFailureCallback = function() {
    ok(false, "Registering a new user failed ...");
    start();
  };

  this.registrationClient.registerUser(this.registrationForm,
  newSuccessCallback, newFailureCallback);
});
```

Testing the WeatherClient object

In the `WeatherClient` object, we will test the following functionalities:

- Getting the weather for a valid location
- Getting the weather for an invalid location (the system should display an error message in this case)

For the time being, this test will not be left for you as an exercise because the other QUnit Ajax testing approach using `asyncTest` will be used for testing the `WeatherClient` object. In order to perform the `WeatherClient` test, `"WeatherClient Test Module"` that groups all the `WeatherClient` tests is created. The following code snippet shows the definition of `"WeatherClient Test Module"`:

```
module("WeatherClient Test Module", {
  setup: function() {

    // The HTML fixture for the WeatherClient.
    document.getElementById("qunit-fixture").innerHTML =
      "<div id=\"weatherInformation\"></div>";

    this.weatherClient = new weatherapp.WeatherClient();

    this.validLocationForm = {
    'location': '1521894',
    'resultDivID': 'weatherInformation'
    };

    this.invalidLocationForm = {
    'location': 'INVALID_LOCATION',
    'resultDivID': 'weatherInformation'
  };
  }, teardown: function() {
    delete this.weatherClient;
    delete this.validLocationForm;
    delete this.invalidLocationForm;
  }
});
```

The `setup` method of `"WeatherClient Test Module"` appends the HTML fixture of the `WeatherClient` test to the `qunit-fixture` div (the HTML fixture contains the `weatherInformation` div element), and then creates an instance from `weatherapp.WeatherClient` creates the `validLocationForm` object that represents a valid location form (that contains a valid location code and the ID of the `weatherInformation` div element), and finally creates the `invalidLocationForm` object that represents an invalid location form (that contains an invalid location code and the ID of the `weatherInformation` div element). The following code snippet shows the `"getting the weather information for a valid place"` test function of `"WeatherClient Test Module"` that tests the `getWeatherCondition` API's behavior with a valid location code:

```
QUnit.config.testTimeout = 10000;
asyncTest("getting the weather information for a valid place",
function() {
  var successCallback = function(response) {
    var resultMessage = response.xmlhttp.responseText;

    notEqual(resultMessage, "", "Getting the weather information
    for a valid place succeeded");
    start();
  };

  var failureCallback = function() {
    ok(false, "Getting the weather information for a valid place
    failed ...");
    start();
  };

  this.weatherClient.getWeatherCondition(this.validLocationForm,
  successCallback, failureCallback);
});
```

In order to test the `getWeatherCondition` method, the `asyncTest` API has been used this time instead of the `test` API. As shown, there are no `stop()` calls because `stop()` is called implicitly by the `asyncTest` API. By calling the `stop()` API implicitly, the `asyncTest` API waits for a call from the `start()` API or it fails the test function after `10000` milliseconds.

Two callbacks are created. The first callback (`successCallback`) represents the success callback while the second one (`failureCallback`) represents the failure callback. Finally, `weatherClient.getWeatherCondition` is called with the valid location form, the success callback, and the failure callback parameters.

In the success callback, the response message returned from the server is ensured of not being equal to an empty message using the `notEqual` assertion (the server response message should contain the weather information for the passed location), and then a call is made to the `start()` API to proceed with the test.

In the failure callback, `ok(false)` is called in order to fail the test function because the failure callback must not be called in case you want to get weather information for a valid location. Finally, a call is made to the `start()` API to proceed with the test.

The following code snippet shows the other `"getting the weather information for an invalid place"` test function of `"WeatherClient Test Module"`:

```
asyncTest("getting the weather information for an invalid place",
function() {
  var successCallback = function() {
    ok(false, "Getting the weather information for an invalid
    place succeeded (MUST NOT Happen)!!!");
    start();
  };

  var failureCallback = function(response) {
    var resultMessage = response.xmlhttp.responseText;

    equal(resultMessage, "Invalid location code", "Getting the
    weather information for an invalid place failed (Expected)
    ...");
    start();
  };

  this.weatherClient.getWeatherCondition(this.invalidLocationForm,
  successCallback, failureCallback);
});
```

As shown in the previous code snippet, the `"getting the weather information for an invalid place"` test function follows the same approach as that of the previous test function. The main difference is that it ensures that `failureCallback` is called and the server response message is validated to be `"Invalid location code"`, and finally it is ensured that `successCallback` is not called.

Running the weather application tests

In order to run the weather application tests correctly, you have to make sure that the server is up and running in order to pass the Ajax tests. So you need to deploy this chapter's updated version of the weather application on Tomcat 6, as explained in *Chapter 1, Unit Testing JavaScript Applications,* and then type the following URL in the browser's address bar:

```
http://localhost:8080/weatherApplication/js/js-test/qunit/testRunner.
html
```

The following screenshot shows the weather application's QUnit test results:

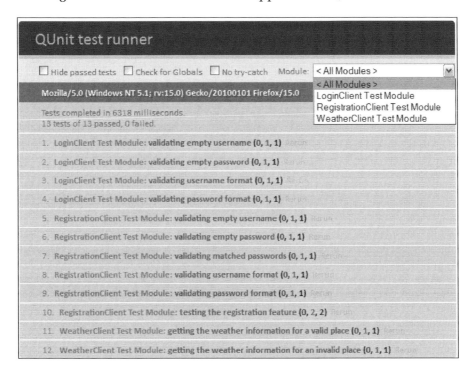

As shown in the preceding screenshot, the test modules appear in the drop-down menu in the top-right part of the test page. You can filter which test modules you want to execute using this drop-down menu; for example, if you select the **LoginClient Test Module** menu item, only the `LoginClient` test functions will be executed, as with the other test modules.

Summary

In this chapter, you learned what QUnit is and how to use it for testing synchronous JavaScript code. You learned how to test asynchronous (Ajax) JavaScript code using the QUnit `test` and QUnit `asyncTest` mechanisms. You learned the assertions provided by the framework, and how to develop your own assertion in order to simplify your test code. You also learned how to load HTML fixtures easily in your QUnit tests. Finally, you learned how to apply all of these concepts for testing the weather application using QUnit. In the next chapter, you will learn how to work with the JsTestDriver framework, and learn how to use it for testing the JavaScript part of the weather application. Along with this, you will also learn how to automate the QUnit and Jasmine tests using the JsTestDriver framework.

5
JsTestDriver

JsTestDriver (JSTD) is one of the most powerful and efficient JavaScript unit testing frameworks. JSTD is not only a JavaScript unit testing framework but also a complete test runner that can run other JavaScript unit testing frameworks, such as Jasmine, YUI Test, and QUnit. JSTD provides a simple syntax for creating JavaScript test cases that can run either from the browser or from the command line; JSTD provides a clean mechanism for testing asynchronous (Ajax) JavaScript code. If you are familiar with the syntax of xUnit frameworks (such as JUnit), you will find yourself familiar with the JSTD syntax. In this chapter, the JSTD framework will be illustrated in detail and will be used to test the weather application that was discussed in *Chapter 1, Unit Testing JavaScript Applications*.

Architecture

Before understanding how to configure JSTD, we need to first understand how it works. The following figure shows the architecture of JsTestDriver:

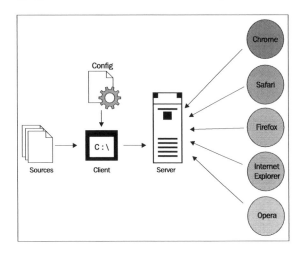

In the first step, the server is launched; then, the server loads the test runner code in the different browsers once they are captured. (A browser can be captured through the command line or by entering the server URL in the browser's address bar. Once the browser is captured, it is called a **slave browser** and can be controlled from the command line.) By sending commands to slave browsers, the server loads the JavaScript code, executes the test cases on every slave browser, and finally returns the results to the client.

We can supply the two following main inputs to the client (command line):

- **JavaScript files**: The JavaScript source and test files (and maybe other helper files)

- A **configuration file**, JsTestDriver.conf: To organize the loading of the JavaScript source and test files

This architecture is flexible; it allows a single server to capture any number of browsers whether they are on the same machine or on different machines on the network. For example, this can be useful if your code is running on a Linux environment and you want to run your JavaScript tests against Microsoft Internet Explorer on another Windows machine.

Configuration

In order to configure JSTD, you need to follow the ensuing steps:

1. Download the framework from http://code.google.com/p/js-test-driver/downloads/list. At the time of this writing, the latest release of JSTD is v1.3.4.b. So, the JsTestDriver-1.3.4.b.jar file has been used for working with JSTD in this chapter.

 As recommended in the previous chapters, it is a good habit to separate the JavaScript source and testing files in different folders for the sake of organization.

2. The second step is to create the JSTD test configuration file, jsTestDriver.conf, as shown in the following code snippet:

```
server: http://localhost:9876

load:
  - src/*.js
  - tests/*.js
```

The configuration file is in **YAML** format (YAML is a recursive acronym for **YAML Ain't Markup Language**. For more information about the YAML format, check `http://yaml.org/`.). The `server` directive refers to the JSTD server URL. If the `server` directive is not specified, the server URL will be needed to be specified at the command line. The `load` directive refers to the JavaScript files to be loaded by the JSTD test runner in order. In the previous code snippet, the `load` directive tells the test runner to load all JavaScript source files with the extension pattern (`*.js`) under the `src` folder and then to load all the JavaScript test files with the same extension pattern, but under the `tests` folder.

3. After creating the JSTD test configuration file, you can now start the server from the command line using the following command:

    ```
    java -jar JsTestDriver-1.3.4.b.jar --port 9876
    ```

    Using this command, the server starts up on port 9876. Once the server starts, you can capture the browsers by entering the following server URL in the browser's address bar:

    ```
    http://localhost:9876/capture
    ```

    In the server startup command, you have the option of launching captured (slave) browsers as follows:

    ```
    java -jar JsTestDriver-1.3.4.b.jar --port 9876 --browser [firefoxp
    ath],[iepath],[chromepath]
    ```

    Using the `browser` argument, you can launch already captured browsers for the server to execute the JavaScript tests on.

4. After you start the server and capture the browsers (manually or from the command line), you can execute the JSTD tests from the command line using the following command:

    ```
    java -jar JsTestDriver-1.3.4.b.jar --tests all
    ```

> Sometimes, you may face the following error while executing the tests:
>
> ```
> "java.lang.RuntimeException: Oh Snap! No server
> defined!"
> ```
>
> This error occurs because JsTestDriver is unable to see the configuration file; in order to avoid this error, you can specify the configuration file path using the `--config` parameter in the command to execute tests, as follows:
>
> ```
> java -jar JsTestDriver-1.3.4.b.jar --config jsTestDriver.
> conf --tests all
> ```

After executing the JSTD tests, you will see the following result in the console if you have executed three successful tests (for example):

```
. . . . . . .
Total 3 tests (Passed: 3; Fails: 0; Errors: 0) (2.00 ms)
Firefox 15.0 Windows: Run 3 tests (Passed: 3; Fails: 0; Errors 0) (2.00
ms)
… Other browsers here …
```

> In order to have the `java` command available from the command line, you need to install and configure Java on your machine. It is expected that you have already installed the JRE as indicated in *Chapter 1, Unit Testing JavaScript Applications*, in order to run the Tomcat server. After installing the JRE, all you need to do to have the `java` command available from your command line is to add the JRE `bin` directory to the PATH variable of your operating system.

Writing your first JSTD test

A JSTD test can contain test cases and test functions. A JSTD test case is a group of related test functions. Every test function should contain one or more assertions in order to perform the test and verify the outputs. The JSTD `TestCase` object is responsible for creating the JSTD test case, and in order to create the test functions inside the test case, every test function should start with the word "test".

Every JSTD assertion represents a function that validates a condition that can return true or false. In order to pass the test function, all of the assertions inside the test function have to be true. If one or more assertions inside a test function are false, the test function fails. The following code snippet shows an example of two JSTD test cases with test functions:

```
TestCase1 = TestCase("Testcase1");

TestCase1.prototype.testFunction1 = function() {
  // One or more assertion(s)
};

TestCase1.prototype.testFunction2 = function() {
  // One or more assertion(s)
};

TestCase2 = TestCase("Testcase2");
```

```
TestCase2.prototype.testAnotherFunction = function() {
  // One or more assertion(s)
};
```

As shown in the preceding code snippet, two test cases are created. The first test case is named Testcase1, and it contains two test functions testFunction1 and testFunction2. The second test case is named Testcase2, and it contains a single test function named testAnotherFunction.

Now, let's move to testing the SimpleMath JavaScript object (which we tested using Jasmine, YUI Test, and QUnit in the previous chapters). The following code snippet reminds you with the code of the SimpleMath object:

```
SimpleMath = function() {
};

SimpleMath.prototype.getFactorial = function (number) {

  if (number < 0) {
    throw new Error("There is no factorial for negative numbers");
  }
  else if (number == 1 || number == 0) {

    // If number <= 1 then number! = 1.
      return 1;
  } else {

    // If number > 1 then number! = number * (number-1)!
      return number * this.getFactorial(number-1);
  }
}

SimpleMath.prototype.signum = function (number) {
    if (number > 0)  {
    return 1;
  } else if (number == 0) {
    return 0;
  } else {
    return -1;
  }
}

SimpleMath.prototype.average = function (number1, number2) {
    return (number1 + number2) / 2;
}
```

As was done in the previous chapters, the following three test scenarios will be developed for the `getFactorial` method:

- A positive number
- Zero
- A negative number

The following code snippet shows how to test calculating the factorial of a positive number (3), 0, and a negative number (-10) by using JSTD:

```
FactorialTestCase = TestCase("Factorial Testcase");

FactorialTestCase.prototype.setUp = function() {
  this.simpleMath = new SimpleMath();
};

FactorialTestCase.prototype.tearDown = function() {
  delete this.simpleMath;
};

FactorialTestCase.prototype.testPositiveNumber = function() {
  assertEquals("Factorial(3)", 6,
  this.simpleMath.getFactorial(3));
};

FactorialTestCase.prototype.testZero = function() {
  assertEquals("Factorial(0)", 1,
  this.simpleMath.getFactorial(0));
};

FactorialTestCase.prototype.testNegativeNumber = function() {
  var localThis = this;

  assertException("Factorial(-10)", function() {
          localThis.simpleMath.getFactorial(-10)
        }, "Error");
};
```

The `TestCase` object declares a new test case called `"Factorial Testcase"`. The `setUp` method is used to initialize the test functions in the test case, that is, the `setUp` method is called once before the run of each test function in the test case. In the `setUp` method, the `simpleMath` object is created using `new SimpleMath()`. On the contrary, the `tearDown` method is used to de-initialize the test functions in the test case; the `tearDown` method is called once after the run of each test function in the test case. In the factorial tests, the `tearDown` method is used to clean up, which deletes the created `simpleMath` object.

In the `testPositiveNumber` test function, the `assertEquals` assertion function calls `simpleMath.getFactorial(3)` and expects the result to be 6. If `simpleMath.getFactorial(3)` returns a value other than 6, the test fails. The first parameter of the `assertEquals` assertion is optional, and it represents a message to be displayed when the assertion fails. In JSTD, we have many other assertions to use instead of `assertEquals`; we will discuss them in greater detail in the *Assertions* section.

In the `testZero` test function, the `assertEquals` assertion function calls `simpleMath.getFactorial(0)` and expects it to be 1. In the `testNegativeNumber` test function, the `assertEquals` assertion function calls `simpleMath.getFactorial(-10)` and expects it to throw an error by using the `assertException` assertion. In JSTD, the `assertException` assertion has three parameters; the first parameter is optional and represents a message to be displayed when the assertion fails, the second parameter represents a callback that contains the function to be tested (which must throw an error in order to make the test function pass), and the last parameter represents the string of the error type.

After finalizing the `getFactorial` test case, we come to a new test case that tests the functionality of the `signum` method provided by the `SimpleMath` object. The following code snippet shows the signum test case:

```
SignumTestCase = TestCase("Signum Testcase");

SignumTestCase.prototype.setUp = function() {
  this.simpleMath = new SimpleMath();
};

SignumTestCase.prototype.tearDown = function() {
  delete this.simpleMath;
};

SignumTestCase.prototype.testPositiveNumber = function() {
  assertEquals("Signum(3)", 1, this.simpleMath.signum(3));
};

SignumTestCase.prototype.testZero = function() {
  assertEquals("Signum(0)", 0, this.simpleMath.signum(0));
};

SignumTestCase.prototype.testNegativeNumber = function() {
  assertEquals("Signum(-1000)", -1, this.simpleMath.signum(-1000));
};
```

We have three test functions for the `signum` method, the `testPositiveNumber` function tests getting the signum of a positive number, the `testZero` function tests getting the signum of zero, and the `testNegativeNumber` function tests getting the signum of a negative number. The following code snippet shows the test case of the `average` method:

```
AverageTestCase = TestCase("Average Testcase");
AverageTestCase.prototype.setUp = function() {
   this.simpleMath = new SimpleMath();
};

AverageTestCase.prototype.tearDown = function() {
   delete this.simpleMath;
};

AverageTestCase.prototype.testAverage = function() {
   assertEquals("Average(3, 6)", 4.5, this.simpleMath.average(3, 6));
};
```

In `"Average Testcase"`, the `testAverage` test function ensures that the average is calculated correctly by calling the `average` method, using the two parameters 3 and 6, and expecting the result to be 4.5.

Note that the first optional message parameter in the JSTD assertions will be displayed if the assertion fails in a way that gives an error with a descriptive meaning. Let's assume that `getFactorial(3)` is returning a wrong value (for example, 10). This means that the following assertion will fail:

```
assertEquals("Factorial(3)", 6, this.simpleMath.getFactorial(3));
```

The result of running this failing assertion will be:

```
Factorial Testcase.testPositiveNumber failed (1.00 ms): AssertError:
Factorial(3) expected 6 but was 10
```

If the first message parameter is omitted, the result will be:

```
Factorial Testcase.testPositiveNumber failed (1.00 ms): AssertError:
expected 6 but was 10
```

In order to run the `SimpleMath` JSTD tests, you need to create the JSTD test configuration file that points to the source and test JavaScript files, and the server URL, as follows:

```
server: http://localhost:9876
load:
  - src/*.js
  - tests/*.js
```

The `simpleMath.js` file is placed under the `src` folder, and the `simpleMathTest.js` file which contains the `SimpleMath` JSTD tests is placed under the `tests` folder. The `load` directive asks the JSTD test runner to load all of the JavaScript files (`*.js`) under the `src` folder and then to load all of the JavaScript files under the `tests` folder in order to execute the JSTD tests.

Then, start the server from the command line by using the following command:

```
java -jar JsTestDriver-1.3.4.b.jar --port 9876
```

Then, capture the browsers (for example, IE and Firefox) by entering the following URL in the browser's address bar:

```
http://localhost:9876/capture
```

Finally, you can execute the tests after you start the server and capture the browsers manually (or from the command line) by using the following command:

```
java -jar JsTestDriver-1.3.4.b.jar --tests all
```

After executing the test cases, you will find the following results in the console:

```
. . . . . . . . . . . . .
Total 14 tests (Passed: 14; Fails: 0; Errors: 0) (8.00 ms)
Microsoft Internet Explorer 8.0 Windows: Run 7 tests (Passed: 7; Fails:
0; Errors 0) (0.00 ms)
Firefox 15.0.1 Windows: Run 7 tests (Passed: 7; Fails: 0; Errors 0) (8.00
ms)
```

Assertions

An assertion is a function that validates a condition; if the condition is not valid, it throws an error that causes the test to fail. A test method can include one or more assertions; all the assertions have to pass in order to have the test method pass. In the first JSTD test example, we have used the `assertEquals` and `assertException` assertions. In this section, the other different built-in assertions provided by JSTD will be illustrated.

The assert, assertTrue, and assertFalse([msg], expression) assertions

The `assert` and `assertTrue` assertions do the same thing; they have two parameters. The first parameter is an optional message to be displayed if the assertion fails, and the second parameter represents an expression. The `assert` and `assertTrue` assertions are passed if the expression parameter is evaluated to `true`. The `assertFalse` assertion does the reverse operation; it passes if the expression is evaluated to false. For example, the following assertions work:

```
assert(6 == 6);
assertTrue("6 should equal 6", 6 == 6);
assertFalse(6 != 6);
```

The assertEquals and assertNotEquals([msg], expected, actual) assertions

The `assertEquals` assertion has three parameters; the first parameter is an optional message to be displayed if the assertion fails, and the last two parameters represent the expected and actual values. The `assertEquals` assertion is passed if the actual value is equal to the expected value; if it is not, the assertion fails and the optional message is displayed. The `assertNotEquals` assertion ensures that the actual and expected parameters are not equal.

It is very important to know that the `assertEquals` and `assertNotEquals` assertions use the JavaScript `==` operator to perform the comparison, that is, they carry out the comparison neglecting the types. For example, the following assertions will be passed:

```
assertEquals("6 should equal '6'", 6, "6");
assertNotEquals("6 should not equal 7", 6, 7);
```

The assertSame and assertNotSame([msg], expected, actual) assertions

The `assertSame` and `assertNotSame` assertions are very similar to the `assertEquals` and `assertNotEquals` assertions. The main difference between them is that the `assertSame` and `assertNotSame` assertions use the `===` operator for comparison, that is, they compare both the values and the types of the actual and expected parameters. For example, the following assertions will be passed:

```
assertSame("6 is the same as 6", 6, 6);
assertNotSame("6 is not the same as '6'", 6, "6");
```

The datatype assertions

The following set of assertions in JSTD checks the value types. Each one of these assertions takes two parameters; the first parameter is an optional message to be displayed if the assertion fails, and the second parameter is the value to be tested:

- `assertBoolean([msg], actual)` is passed if the actual value is a Boolean
- `assertString([msg], actual)` is passed if the actual value is a string
- `assertNumber([msg], actual)` is passed if the actual value is a number
- `assertArray([msg], actual)` is passed if the actual value is an array
- `assertFunction([msg], actual)` is passed if the actual value is a function
- `assertObject([msg], actual)` is passed if the actual value is an object

For example, the following assertions will be passed:

```
assertBoolean(false);
assertString("some string");
assertNumber(1000);
assertArray([1, 2, 3]);
assertFunction(function(){ alert('test'); });
assertObject({somekey: 'someValue'});
```

JSTD also provides generic assertions, `assertTypeOf` and `assertInstanceOf`, for checking the datatypes.

The `assertTypeOf` assertion uses the JavaScript `typeof` operator in order to check the value type. It takes three parameters; the first parameter is an optional message to be displayed if the assertion fails, and the other two parameters represent the value type and the value to test. For example, the following `assertTypeOf` assertions will pass:

```
assertTypeOf("boolean", false);
assertTypeOf("string", "some string");
assertTypeOf("number", 1000);
assertTypeOf("object", [1, 2, 3]);
assertTypeOf("function", function(){ alert('test'); });
assertTypeOf("object", {somekey: 'someValue'});
```

In addition to all of this, you can use the `assertInstanceOf` assertion, which uses the JavaScript `instanceof` operator in order to check the value instance. It takes three parameters; the first parameter is an optional message to be displayed if the assertion fails, and the other two parameters represent the type constructor and the value to be tested. For example, the following assertions will pass:

```
assertInstanceOf(Boolean, false);
assertInstanceOf(String, "some string");
assertInstanceOf(Number, 1000);
assertInstanceOf(Object, [1, 2, 3]);
assertInstanceOf(Function, function(){ alert('test'); });
assertInstanceOf(Object, {somekey: 'someValue'});
```

Special value assertions

The following set of assertions in JSTD checks whether a variable value belongs to one of the special values as mentioned in the following list. Each one of these assertions takes two parameters; the first parameter is an optional message to be displayed if the assertion fails, and the second parameter is the value to be tested:

- `assertUndefined([msg], actual)` is passed if the actual value is undefined
- `assertNotUndefined([msg], actual)` is passed if the actual value is not undefined (defined)
- `assertNull([msg], actual)` is passed if the actual value is null
- `assertNotNull([msg], actual)` is passed if the actual value is not null
- `assertNaN([msg], actual)` is passed if the actual value is not a number (NaN)
- `assertNotNaN([msg], actual)` is passed if the actual value is not NaN

For example, the following assertions will be passed:

```
var someStr = "some string";
var undefinedVar;

assertUndefined(undefinedVar);
assertNotUndefined(someStr);
assertNull(null);
assertNotNull(someStr);
assertNaN(1000 / "string_value");
assertNotNaN(1000);
```

The fail([msg]) assertion

In some situations, you may need to fail the test manually, for example, if you want to make your own custom assertion that encapsulates specific validation logic. In order to do this, JSTD provides the `fail()` method for failing the test manually. `assertAverage` is an example of a custom assertion that uses the `fail()` method:

```
assertAverage = function (number1, number2, expected, failureMessage)
{
  var actual = (number1 + number2) / 2;

  if (actual != expected) {
    fail(failureMessage + ": Expected = " + expected + " while
    Actual = " + actual);
  }
}
```

The `assertAverage` custom assertion can be called by simply using the following line of code:

```
assertAverage(3, 4, 3.5, "Average is incorrect");
```

The `fail()` method has an optional message parameter that is displayed as a failure message.

 There are other remaining built-in assertions in JSTD; however, the only remaining important built-in assertion that you have to know is `assertException`, and you already learned how it works in the `SimpleMath` object test example.

Testing asynchronous (Ajax) JavaScript code

The common question that comes to mind is how to test asynchronous (Ajax) JavaScript code using JSTD. What has been mentioned in the chapter so far is how to perform unit testing for the synchronous JavaScript code. Fortunately, JSTD provides the `AsyncTestCase` object in order to perform asynchronous JavaScript testing (Ajax testing). In the following section, you will understand how to work with the `AsyncTestCase` object in order to develop asynchronous tests in JSTD.

AsyncTestCase, queue, and callbacks

AsyncTestCase extends TestCase by allowing the test methods to have a queue parameter. The queue parameter can contain a list of inline functions (steps) that are executed in sequence. Every inline function has a callbacks parameter that allows creating different callbacks for testing the asynchronous operations. JSTD mainly has two types of callbacks:

- **Success callbacks**: These represent the success path. The success callback must be called if the Ajax operation succeeds. In order to handle the operation timeout, if the success callback is not called after a specific amount of time (30 seconds, by default), the test function fails.

- **Error callbacks**: These represent the error path. The error callback must not be called if the Ajax operation succeeds. If the error callback is called, the test function fails.

 The JSTD queue parameter contains a list of inline functions that are executed in sequence, which is helpful if you want to test a group of dependent Ajax operations.

The following code snippet shows an example of real Ajax testing using JSTD:

```
AsynchronousTestCase = AsyncTestCase("Asynchronous Testcase");

AsynchronousTestCase.prototype.testAjaxOperationsGroup1 =
function(queue) {
  queue.call('Testing operation1 ...', function(callbacks) {
      var successCallback =
      callbacks.add(function(successParameters) {
      // Make the assertions for the successParameters...
        });

      var failureCallback = callbacks.addErrback('Unable to
      register the user');

      // call asynchronous API
      asyncSystem.doAjaxOperation(inputData, successCallback,
      failureCallback);
  });

  queue.call('Testing operation2 ...', function(callbacks) {
    // will be called after 'Testing operation1 ...'
  });
};
```

```
AsynchronousTestCase.prototype.testAjaxOperationsGroup2 =
function(queue) {
  //...
};
```

As shown in the preceding code snippet, an asynchronous test case, `"Asynchronous Testcase"`, is created. It has two test methods: `testAjaxOperationsGroup1` and `testAjaxOperationsGroup2`. Every test method has a `queue` parameter. In the `testAjaxOperationsGroup1` test method, the `queue` object includes two inline functions, `"Testing operation1 ..."` and `"Testing operation2 ..."`, using the `queue.call()` API.

 The `queue.call()` API has two parameters; the first parameter is optional and represents the title of the inline function, and the second parameter represents the inline function.

Every inline function has a `callbacks` parameter. The `callbacks` parameter allows creating the success and failure callbacks in order to test and validate the Ajax operations. In the `"Testing operation1 ..."` inline function, two callbacks are created; one of them is the success callback (`successCallback`) and it is called if the Ajax operation succeeds. The success callback is created using the `callbacks.add()` API. The other callback is the failure callback (`failureCallback`), and it is called if the Ajax operation fails. The failure callback is created using the `callbacks.addErrback()` API.

If the Ajax response is not returned from the server after 30 seconds, the success callback will cause the test to fail. In the next section, the `AsyncTestCase`, `queue`, and `callbacks` objects will be used in order to test the (asynchronous) Ajax part of the weather application.

Testing the weather application

Now, we come to developing the JSTD tests for our weather application. Actually, after you know how to write JSTD tests for both synchronous and asynchronous JavaScript (Ajax) code, testing the weather application is an easy task. As you remember from the previous chapters, we have three major JavaScript objects in the weather application that we need to develop tests for: the `LoginClient`, `RegistrationClient`, and `WeatherClient` objects.

Two subfolders, `jstd` and `tests`, are created under the `js-test` folder
(thus: `jstd\tests`) to contain the JSTD tests, as shown in the following screenshot:

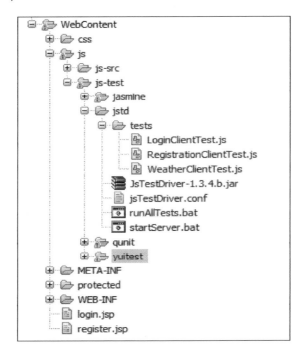

As shown in the preceding screenshot, there are three JSTD test files
(`LoginClientTest.js`, `RegistrationClientTest.js`, and `WeatherClientTest.
js`) that test the main three JavaScript objects of the weather application.

> Using the JSTD DOC annotation, you can load the HTML fixtures (in
> an inline style) in your JSTD tests. For example:
> ```
> FixtureTestCase = TestCase("Fixture Testcase");
> FixtureTestCase.prototype.testSomeThing = function()
> {
>   /*:DOC += <div id="someDiv"></div> */
>   assertNotNull(document.getElementById('someDiv'));
> };
> ```

Testing the LoginClient object

As we did in the previous chapters, in the *Testing the LoginClient object* section we will perform unit testing for the following functionalities:

- Validation of empty username and password
- Validating that the username is in e-mail address format
- Validating that the password contains at least one digit, one capital and small letter, at least one special character, and six characters or more

In order to perform this test, one test case is created that tests both the validation of the empty fields (the username and password) and the validation of the fields' formats. The following code snippet shows the validation of the empty fields for `"LoginClient Testcase"`:

```
LoginClientTestcase = TestCase("LoginClient Testcase");

LoginClientTestcase.prototype.setUp = function() {
  /*:DOC += <label for="username">Username  <span
  id="usernameMessage" class="error"></span></label>
   <input type="text" id="username" name="username"/>
   <label for="password">Password  <span id="passwordMessage"
   class="error"></span></label>
   <input type="password" id="password" name="password"/>*/

  this.loginClient = new weatherapp.LoginClient();

    this.loginForm = {
    "userNameField" : "username",
     "passwordField" : "password",
     "userNameMessage" : "usernameMessage",
     "passwordMessage" : "passwordMessage"
    };
};

LoginClientTestcase.prototype.tearDown = function() {
  delete this.loginClient;
  delete this.loginForm;
};

LoginClientTestcase.prototype.testEmptyUserName = function() {
  document.getElementById("username").value = ""; /* setting
  username to empty */
  document.getElementById("password").value = "Admin@123";
```

```
        this.loginClient.validateLoginForm(this.loginForm);

        assertEquals("(field is required)",
        document.getElementById("usernameMessage").innerHTML);
    };

    LoginClientTestcase.prototype.testEmptyPassword = function() {
        document.getElementById("username").value = "someone@yahoo.com";
        document.getElementById("password").value = "";   /* setting
        password to empty */

        this.loginClient.validateLoginForm(this.loginForm);

        assertEquals("(field is required)",
        document.getElementById("passwordMessage").innerHTML);
    };
```

The setUp method creates an instance from weatherapp.LoginClient and creates the loginForm object, which holds the IDs of the HTML elements that are used in the test. The HTML fixture of LoginClientTestCase is loaded using the DOC annotation.

testEmptyUserName tests whether the LoginClient object is able to display an error message when the username is not entered. It sets an empty value in the username field and then calls the validateLoginForm API of the LoginClient object. It then checks whether the validateLoginForm API produces the "(field is required)" message in the usernameMessage field by using the assertEquals assertion.

testEmptyPassword does the same thing, but with the password field, not with the username field.

The following code snippet shows the second part of "LoginClient Testcase", which validates the formats of the fields (username and password):

```
    LoginClientTestcase.prototype.testUsernameFormat = function() {
        document.getElementById("username").value =
        "someone@someDomain";   /* setting username to invalid format */
        document.getElementById("password").value = "Admin@123";

        this.loginClient.validateLoginForm(this.loginForm);

        assertEquals("(format is invalid)",
        document.getElementById("usernameMessage").innerHTML);
    };

    LoginClientTestcase.prototype.testPasswordFormat = function() {
        document.getElementById("username").value =
```

```
    "someone@someDomain.com";
    document.getElementById("password").value = "Admin123"; /*
    setting password to invalid format */

    this.loginClient.validateLoginForm(this.loginForm);

    assertEquals("(format is invalid)",
    document.getElementById("passwordMessage").innerHTML);
};
```

testUsernameFormat tests the validation of the username format. It tests whether the LoginClient object is able to display an error message when the username format is not valid. It sets an invalid e-mail value in the username field and then calls the validateLoginForm API of the LoginClient object. Finally, it checks, by using the assertEquals assertion, whether the validateLoginForm API produces the "(format is invalid)" message in the usernameMessage field.

testPasswordFormat enters a password that does not comply with the application's password rules—it enters a password that does not include a capital letter—and then calls the validateLoginForm API of the LoginClient object. Finally, it checks whether the validateLoginForm API produces the "(format is invalid)" message in the passwordMessage field.

Testing the RegistrationClient object

In the RegistrationClient object, we will test the following functionalities:

- Validation of empty username and passwords
- Validation of matched passwords
- Validating that the username is in e-mail address format
- Validating that the password contains at least one digit, one capital and small letter, at least one special character, and six characters or more
- Validating that the user registration Ajax functionality is performed correctly

Testing of the first four functionalities will be skipped because they are pretty similar to the tests that are explained in the LoginClient test case, so let's explain how to check whether the user registration (registerUser) Ajax functionality is performed correctly.

The `registerUser` test case should cover the following test scenarios:

- Testing adding a new user, that is, the registration client should be able to register a valid user correctly.
- Testing adding a user with an existing user ID (username). In this case, the registration client should fail when registering a user whose ID is already registered.

The `RegistrationTestcase` asynchronous test case is created in order to validate the user registration Ajax functionality. The following code snippet shows the first part of the `RegistrationTestcase` test case, which tests adding a new user. The `setUp` method creates an instance from `weatherapp.RegistrationClient` and creates the `registrationForm` object, which holds the IDs of the registration form that will be used in the test. Using the DOC annotation, the HTML fixture of `RegistrationTestcase` is loaded:

```
RegistrationTestcase = AsyncTestCase("Registration Testcase");

RegistrationTestcase.prototype.setUp = function() {
  /*:DOC += <label for="username">Username (Email)  <span
  id="usernameMessage" class="error"></span></label>
  <input type="text" id="username" name="username"/>
  <label for="password1">Password  <span id="passwordMessage1"
  class="error"></span></label>
  <input type="password" id="password1" name="password1"/>
  <label for="password2">Confirm your password</label>
  <input type="password" id="password2" name="password2"/>*/

  this.registrationClient = new weatherapp.RegistrationClient();

  this.registrationForm = {
      "userNameField" : "username",
      "passwordField1" : "password1",
      "passwordField2" : "password2",
      "userNameMessage" : "usernameMessage",
      "passwordMessage1" : "passwordMessage1"
    };
};

RegistrationTestcase.prototype.tearDown = function() {
  delete this.registrationClient;
  delete this.registrationForm;
};
```

```
RegistrationTestcase.prototype.testRegisterUser = function(queue) {
  var this_local = this;

  queue.call('Registering a new user ...', function(callbacks) {
    this_local.userName = "hazems" + new Date().getTime() +
    "@apache.org";

    document.getElementById("username").value =
    this_local.userName;
    document.getElementById("password1").value = "Admin@123";
    document.getElementById("password2").value = "Admin@123";

      var successCallback = callbacks.add(function(response) {
        var resultMessage = response.xmlhttp.responseText;
        assertEquals("User is registered successfully ...",
        resultMessage);

        jstestdriver.console.log("[Success] User is registered
        successfully ...");
        });

      var failureCallback = callbacks.addErrback('Unable to
      register the user');

      // call asynchronous API
  this_local.registrationClient.registerUser(this_local.
  registrationForm, successCallback, failureCallback);
    });

  //...
};
```

In the `testRegisterUser` test method, an inline function (`'Registering a new user ...'`), tests the creation of a new user using `queue.call()`. The registration form is filled with a valid generated username and valid matched passwords, and then two callbacks are created using the `callbacks` parameter. `successCallback` which represents the success callback, while `failureCallback` represents the failure callback. `registrationClient.registerUser` is called with the registration form, the success callback, and the failure callback parameters. The `'Registering a new user ...'` inline test function waits for a call to either the success or failure callback, or it fails after the timeout period passes.

In `successCallback`, the callback checks whether the returned response message from the server is `"User is registered successfully ..."` using the `assertEquals` assertion. The failure callback displays the `"Unable to register the user"` message if the `registerUser` test case fails.

> The `jstestdriver.console.log` API can be used for JSTD logging in the console. In the example, it is used to display the "operation successful" message.

The following code snippet shows the second inline function, `'Registering a user whose id is already existing ...'`, of the `testRegisterUser` test method. It tests registering a user with an existing ID:

```
queue.call('Registering a user whose id is already existing ...',
function(callbacks) {
  document.getElementById("username").value = this_local.userName;
  document.getElementById("password1").value = "Admin@123";
  document.getElementById("password2").value = "Admin@123";

  var failureCallback = callbacks.add(function(response) {
    var resultMessage = response.xmlhttp.responseText;
    assertEquals("A user with the same username is already registered
    ...", resultMessage);

    jstestdriver.console.log("[Success] User is not created because
    the user id is already registered ...");
  });

  var successCallback = callbacks.addErrback('[Error] A user with the
  same id is created !!!');

  // call asynchronous API
  this_local.registrationClient.registerUser(this_local.
registrationForm, successCallback, failureCallback);
});
```

The registration form is filled with the existing user ID (that is already registered in the first inline test function) and with a valid password, and the failure and the success callbacks are created. Then, `registrationClient.registerUser` is called with the registration form, the success callback, and the failure callback parameters.

In the failure callback (which must be called if the `registerUser` test case works correctly), the callback checks whether the returned response message from the server is `"A user with the same username is already registered ..."`, using the `assertEquals` assertion. The success callback displays the `"[Error] A user with the same id is created !!!"` message if the `registerUser` test case creates a new user with an existing user ID.

Testing the WeatherClient object

In the `WeatherClient` object, we will unit test the following functionalities:

- Getting the weather for a valid location
- Getting the weather for an invalid location (the system should display an error message for this case)

To test the `WeatherClient` object, the same technique that we used in the `registerUser` test case is followed. Developing this test will be left for you as an exercise; you can get the full source code of the `WeatherClientTest.js` file from the `Chapter 5` folder in the code bundle available on the book's website. To view the source code for the JavaScript tests, all you need to do is unzip the `weatherApplication.zip` file, and you will be able to find all the JSTD tests under `weatherApplication/WebContent/js/js-test/jstd/tests`.

Configuring the proxy

In order to allow sending Ajax requests from the JSTD server to the backend server, we need to access the backend server through a proxy so as to avoid the "security permission denied" error that occurs due to the cross-domain request(s). Fortunately, JSTD provides a gateway (proxy) that can be used for this purpose. The following code snippet shows the complete `JsTestDriver.config` file of the weather application JSTD test:

```
server: http://localhost:9876

gateway:
  - {matcher: "*", server: "http://localhost:8080"}

load:
  - ../../js-src/*.js
  - tests/*.js

plugin:
  - name: "coverage"
    jar: coverage-1.3.4.b.jar
    module: "com.google.jstestdriver.coverage.CoverageModule"
```

In the configuration file, there are two newly introduced directives (that are not explained in the first JSTD test example), the `gateway` and `plugin` directives. The `plugin` directive is used to define a JSTD plugin. For this example, it defines the code coverage plugin that is used to generate the test reports (this plugin will be illustrated in detail in the *Generating test reports* section). The `gateway` directive can be used to route the requests that match the `matcher` attribute's pattern to the corresponding server URL specified in the `server` attribute. For the weather application tests, all of the Ajax requests (which are represented using the "`*`" pattern) will be routed to the backend server in `http://localhost:8080`, which hosts the weather application backend APIs.

> In the matcher attribute, you can use the following varieties of patterns:
> - **Literal matchers**: For example, "`/matchedService`"
> - **Suffix matchers**: For example, "`/matchedService/*`"
> - **Prefix matchers**: For example, "`*.json`"

Running the weather application tests

In order to run the weather application tests correctly, you have to make sure that the Tomcat server is up and running and that this chapter's updated version of the weather application is deployed on the server as explained in *Chapter 1, Unit Testing JavaScript Applications*. After this, you need to follow these steps:

1. Launch the command prompt and change directory (cd) to the "`${INSTALL_PATH}\weatherApplication\WebContent\js\js-test\jstd\`" path in the deployed weather application.

2. Start the JSTD server by typing the command `java -jar JsTestDriver-1.3.4.b.jar --port 9876`.

3. Capture the browsers (for example, Firefox and Internet Explorer) by entering the following URL in the browser's address bar:

   `http://localhost:9876/capture`

4. Finally, run the JSTD test command as follows:

   ```
   java -jar JsTestDriver-1.3.4.b.jar --config jsTestDriver.conf
   --tests all
   ```

The following result snippet shows the output of running the JSTD tests of the weather application:

```
........................
Total 24 tests (Passed: 24; Fails: 0; Errors: 0) (1297.00 ms)

  Microsoft Internet Explorer 8.0 Windows: Run 12 tests (Passed: 12;
  Fails: 0; Errors 0) (610.00 ms)

    Registration Testcase.testRegisterUser passed (32.00 ms)

    [LOG] [Success] User is registered successfully...

    [LOG] [Success] User is not created because the user id is
    already registered...

    WeatherClient Testcase.testGetWeatherForValidPlace passed (328.00
    ms)

    [LOG] [Success] Weather information is retrieved successfully...

    WeatherClient Testcase.testGetWeatherForInvalidPlace passed
    (250.00 ms)

    [LOG] [Success] The weather information is not retrieved for the
    invalid place...

  Firefox 15.0.1 Windows: Run 12 tests (Passed: 12; Fails: 0; Errors
  0) (1297.00 ms)

    Registration Testcase.testRegisterUser passed (493.00 ms)

    [LOG] [Success] User is registered successfully...

    [LOG] [Success] User is not created because the user id is
    already registered...

    WeatherClient Testcase.testGetWeatherForValidPlace passed (539.00
    ms)

    [LOG] [Success] Weather information is retrieved successfully...

    WeatherClient Testcase.testGetWeatherForInvalidPlace passed
    (252.00 ms)

    [LOG] [Success] The weather information is not retrieved for the
    invalid place...
```

Generating test reports

JSTD can generate test reports from the test results by using the code coverage plugin. The code coverage plugin can also produce code coverage files—in the **Linux code coverage (LCOV)** format—which include the test code coverage statistics.

Code coverage is a software testing measure. It shows how much the source code of a program has been tested. It has many criteria for this measurement, for example:

- Line coverage measures the percentage of the program lines that are covered by the test
- Function coverage measures the percentage of the program functions that are covered by the test
- Branch coverage measures the percentage of the program branches (for example, *if ... else*) that are covered by the test

In order to generate the test reports from the JSTD tests, you need to do the following:

1. Download the code coverage plugin file (`coverage-1.3.4.b.jar`) from the download page of JSTD, which can be found at the following location:

   `http://code.google.com/p/js-test-driver/downloads/list`

2. Add the code coverage plugin declaration to the `JsTestDriver.conf` file, as follows:

```
plugin:
  - name: "coverage"
    jar: coverage-1.3.4.b.jar
    module: "com.google.jstestdriver.coverage.CoverageModule"
```

   This declaration tells JSTD to include the plugin whose name is `coverage` from the `com.google.jstestdriver.coverage.CoverageModule` module that resides in the `coverage-1.3.4.b.jar` file.

3. Finally, you need to specify the `--testOutput` parameter in the test running command. The `--testOutput` parameter specifies the path in which JSTD will generate the test report files. For example:

```
java -jar JsTestDriver-1.3.4.b.jar --config jsTestDriver.conf
--tests all --testOutput reports
```

   This command tells JSTD to generate the test reports under the `reports` directory.

The following screenshot shows the generated report files after performing the three preceding steps:

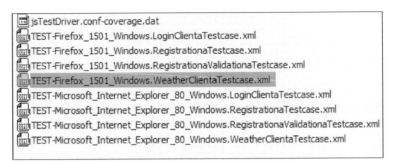

As shown in the preceding screenshot, there are nine generated files. The `jsTestDriver.conf-coverage.dat` file is the generated LCOV file that contains the code coverage statistics (currently, the JSTD code coverage plugin generates the code coverage based on the line coverage criteria). The other eight files are JUnit XML report files that have the following naming format:

```
TEST-[BrowserName_Version_Platform].[TestCaseShortName]Testcase.xml
```

In the weather application, there are four test cases that have four XML files per browser:

- `"LoginClient Testcase"`
- `"Registration Validation Testcase"`
- `"Registration Testcase"`
- `"WeatherClient Testcase"`

As a sample for the generated test report files, the following code snippet shows the `"LoginClient Testcase"` JUnit XML report file for Firefox. The displayed JUnit XML report file is named `TEST-Firefox_1501_Windows.LoginClientaTestcase.xml`.

```
<?xml version="1.0" encoding="UTF-8"?>
<testsuite name="Firefox_1501_Windows.LoginClient Testcase" errors="0"
failures="0" tests="4" time="0.013">
<testcase classname="Firefox_1501_Windows.LoginClient Testcase"
name="testEmptyUserName" time="0.0040"/>
<testcase classname="Firefox_1501_Windows.LoginClient Testcase"
name="testEmptyPassword" time="0.0010"/>
<testcase classname="Firefox_1501_Windows.LoginClient Testcase"
name="testUsernameFormat" time="0.0060"/>
<testcase classname="Firefox_1501_Windows.LoginClient Testcase"
name="testPasswordFormat" time="0.0020"/>
</testsuite>
```

Now, let's learn how to generate user-friendly code coverage reports in JSTD. Fortunately, the JSTD-generated LCOV files can be converted to user-friendly HTML reports using the LCOV visualizer tool that can be found at `http://ltp.sourceforge.net/coverage/lcov.php`.

The LCOV visualizer works on a Red Hat Linux environment. In order to convert the LCOV files to HTML reports, you should do the following:

1. Download the latest LCOV visualizer RPM (`lcov-X.Y-Z.noarch.rpm`) file from `http://ltp.sourceforge.net/coverage/lcov.php`

2. Install the downloaded RPM file in your Red Hat Linux environment by using the following command:

   ```
   rpm -i lcov-1.9-1.noarch.rpm
   ```

3. In order to make sure that the LCOV visualizer tool is installed correctly, type the `genhtml` command at the command line, and you should see the following output:

   ```
   genhtml: No filename specified
   ```

   ```
   Use genhtml --help to get usage information
   ```

4. Run the `genhtml` command on the JSTD-generated LCOV file in order to generate the HTML test coverage report shown in the following screenshot:

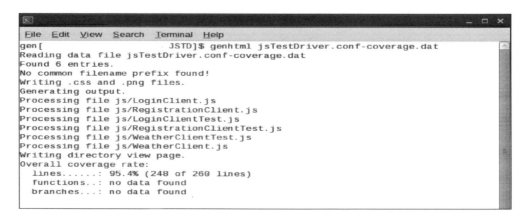

Note that the `jsTestDriver.conf-coverage.dat` file has the format shown in the following code snippet:

```
SF:[PATH]\Workspaces\weatherApplication\WebContent\js\LoginClient.
js
DA:1,2
...
end_of_record
```

```
SF:[PATH]\weatherApplication\WebContent\js\RegistrationClient.js
DA:1,2
...
end_of_record
SF:[PATH]\weatherApplication\WebContent\js\WeatherClient.js
DA:1,2
...
end_of_record
SF:[PATH]\weatherApplication\WebContent\js\LoginClientTest.js
DA:10,2
...
end_of_record
SF:[PATH]\weatherApplication\WebContent\js\RegistrationClientTest.
js
DA:12,2
...
end_of_record
SF:[PATH]\weatherApplication\WebContent\js\WeatherClientTest.js
DA:8,2
...
end_of_record
```

As shown in the LCOV generated file, the generated SF attributes contain the full paths of both the JavaScript source and test files. So, you have to make sure that these paths are updated if you change the location of the JavaScript files.

If you run the genhtml command and the paths of the SF attributes are not correct, you will encounter the following error:

"mkdir: cannot create directory `': No such file or directory

genhtml: ERROR: cannot create directory !"

5. If the `genhtml` command is passed successfully, you will find the generated HTML code coverage report files; click on the `index.html` file to see the HTML report shown in the following screenshot:

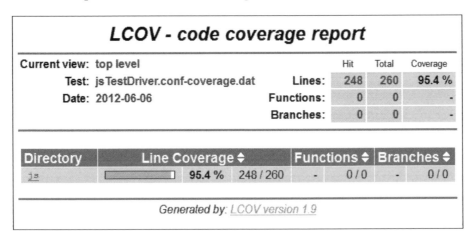

You can drill down in the report by clicking on the `js` directory link to see the test result details of each JavaScript file.

The generated LCOV HTML report is placed under the `lcov-html` folder, which is under the `jstd` folder; you can access the generated HTML report on your Tomcat server by using the following URL:

`http://localhost:8080/weatherApplication/js/js-test/jstd/lcov-html/index.html`

Integration with other JavaScript test frameworks

As we know from the definition of JSTD, it is not only a JavaScript test framework but also a complete test runner that can run other JavaScript frameworks on top of it, using **adapters**. Fortunately, JSTD has many ready-made adapters, developed by the open source community, that enable many JavaScript frameworks (such as Jasmine, QUnit, and YUI Test) to integrate with JSTD. The integration of JSTD with both Jasmine and QUnit is highly required because these testing frameworks do not have an out-of-the-box mechanism for executing the tests from the command-line interface (unlike YUI Test, which can run from the command line using YUI Test Selenium

Driver, as illustrated in detail in *Chapter 3, YUI Test*). Having the ability to execute the tests from the command-line interface allows automating the running of tests by using the build and the continuous integration tools.

In this section, the required steps and tricks that are needed for integrating our previously written Jasmine and QUnit tests (the weather application) with the JSTD runner will be illustrated.

Before digging into the details of this integration, let's see the structure of the `integration` folder, which contains the JSTD-Jasmine and JSTD-QUnit integration files in the weather application:

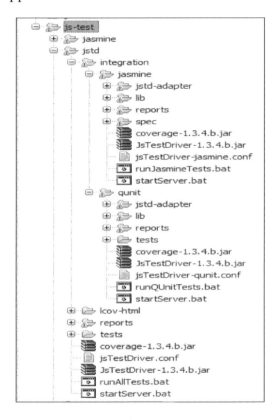

As shown in the preceding screenshot, the `integration` folder contains two subfolders—the `jasmine` folder and the `qunit` folder. The `jasmine` folder and the `qunit` folder each contain the following subfolders:

- `jstd-adapter`: These contain the JSTD adapter files
- `lib`: These contain the JavaScript framework library files (whether Jasmine or QUnit)

- spec and tests: These contain the Jasmine and QUnit test files, respectively
- reports: These contain the report files

The jasmine folder and the qunit folder contain the following files:

- JsTestDriver-1.3.4.b.jar: The JSTD JAR file.
- coverage-1.3.4.b.jar: The JSTD code coverage JAR file.
- jsTestDriver-*.conf: The JSTD configuration files.
- Two batch files that can start the JSTD server and execute the Jasmine (or QUnit) tests. These two files will work with you if you are using Windows; if you are working in a Linux environment, you can create equivalent .sh files to start up the server and execute the tests without having to remember the commands.

Integrating JSTD with Jasmine

In order to integrate the Jasmine tests of the weather application with JSTD, you need to:

1. Download the JasmineAdapter.js file from the following URL:

   https://github.com/ibolmo/jasmine-jstd-adapter/blob/master/src/JasmineAdapter.js

2. Place the downloaded JasmineAdapter.js file under the /integration/jasmine/jstd-adapter folder.

3. Create a configuration file, named jsTestDriver-jasmine.conf, that contains the JSTD-Jasmine configuration, which is shown in the following code snippet:

```
server: http://localhost:9876
gateway:
  - {matcher: "*", server: "http://localhost:8080"}
load:
  - lib/jasmine-1.2.0/jasmine.js
  - lib/plugins/jasmine-jquery/jquery.js
  - jstd-adapter/JasmineAdapter.js
  - lib/plugins/jasmine-jquery/jasmine-jquery.js
  - ../../../../js-src/*.js
  - spec/*.js
plugin:
  - name: "coverage"
    jar: coverage-1.3.4.b.jar
    module: "com.google.jstestdriver.coverage.CoverageModule"
```

In the load directive, you need to load the following files in order:

- ○ The Jasmine framework file
- ○ The jQuery file
- ○ The Jasmine JSTD adapter file
- ○ The Jasmine jQuery plugin file
- ○ The JavaScript source files
- ○ The Jasmine JavaScript test files

This is basically what is needed in order to have Jasmine tests running on top of the JSTD test runner. However, you need to take the loadFixtures API of the Jasmine jQuery plugin into consideration. Due to the changes of the paths between JSTD and Jasmine, the loadFixtures API will not work correctly. In order to run the loading of the fixture correctly, you have two options:

- Replace the loadFixtures API with the jasmine.getFixtures().set API and load the fixtures in an inline style (which is the approach followed in the weather application's JSTD-Jasmine tests)
- Configure the Jasmine loadFixtures API to work with JSTD

In order to configure the loadFixtures API to work with JSTD, you need to do the following:

1. Specify explicitly the fixture path by using jasmine.getFixtures(). fixturesPath, and start the fixture path with /test, as follows:

```
jasmine.getFixtures().fixturesPath = '/test/spec/javascripts/
fixtures/';
loadFixtures("loginFixture.html");
```

2. Load the HTML fixtures using the serve directive in the JSTD-Jasmine configuration file jsTestDriver-jasmine.conf, as shown in the following code snippet:

```
server: http://localhost:9876
gateway:
  - {matcher: "*", server: "http://localhost:8080"}
serve:
  - spec/javascripts/fixtures/*.html
load:
  - lib/jasmine-1.2.0/jasmine.js
  - lib/plugins/jasmine-jquery/jquery.js
  - jstd-adapter/JasmineAdapter.js
  - lib/plugins/jasmine-jquery/jasmine-jquery.js
  - ../../../../js-src/*.js
```

```
      - spec/*.js
  plugin:
      - name: "coverage"
        jar: coverage-1.3.4.b.jar
        module: "com.google.jstestdriver.coverage.CoverageModule"
```

After applying the preceding steps, you can now start the JSTD server as usual, using the following command:

`java -jar JsTestDriver-1.3.4.b.jar --port 9876`

Then, capture two browsers (for example, Firefox and IE) by entering the following URL in the browser's address bar:

`http://localhost:9876/capture`

Finally, you can run the Jasmine tests on top of the JSTD test runner by executing the JSTD test running command:

`java -jar JsTestDriver-1.3.4.b.jar --config jsTestDriver-jasmine.conf --tests all --testOutput reports`

The output in the console will be as follows:

`Total 26 tests (Passed: 26; Fails: 0; Errors: 0) (1538.00 ms)`

`Microsoft Internet Explorer 8.0 Windows: Run 13 tests (Passed: 13; Fails: 0; Errors 0) (922.00 ms)`

`Firefox 15.0.1 Windows: Run 13 tests (Passed: 13; Fails: 0; Errors 0) (1538.00 ms)`

In the `reports` folder under the `/integration/jasmine` folder, you will find 18 JUnit XML report files (nine files for the tests on Firefox and nine for the tests on IE). Every JUnit XML report file contains the test results of a single Jasmine test suite.

Integrating JSTD with QUnit

In order to integrate the QUnit tests of the weather application with JSTD, you need to do the following:

1. Download the `equiv.js` and `QUnitAdapter.js` files from the following URL:

    `https://github.com/exnor/QUnit-to-JsTestDriver-adapter`

2. Place the two downloaded files in the `jstd-adapter` folder under the `/integration/qunit` folder.

3. Create a configuration file, named `jsTestDriver-qunit.conf`, that contains the JSTD-QUnit configuration, which is as shown in the following code snippet:

```
server: http://localhost:9876

gateway:
  - {matcher: "*", server: "http://localhost:8080"}

load:
  - lib/qunit-1.10.0.js
  - jstd-adapter/equiv.js
  - jstd-adapter/QUnitAdapter.js
  - ../../../../js-src/*.js
  - tests/*.js

plugin:
  - name: "coverage"
    jar: coverage-1.3.4.b.jar
    module: "com.google.jstestdriver.coverage.CoverageModule"
```

As you may have noticed in the preceding code snippet, you need to load the following files in order, in the `load` directive:

  ◦ The QUnit framework file
  ◦ The QUnit JSTD adapter files (`equiv.js` and `QUnitAdapter.js`)
  ◦ The JavaScript source files
  ◦ The QUnit JavaScript test files

This is basically what is needed in order to have the QUnit tests working on the top of the JSTD test runner. However, you need to take the loading of HTML fixtures into consideration. In order to load the HTML fixtures in the JSTD-QUnit tests, you can use the standard JSTD DOC annotation shown in the following code snippet:

```
module("LoginClient Test Module", {
  setup: function() {
    /*:DOC += <label for="username">Username   <span
    id="usernameMessage" class="error"></span></label>
    <input type="text" id="username" name="username"/>
    <label for="password">Password   <span id="passwordMessage"
    class="error"></span></label>
    <input type="password" id="password" name="password"/>*/

    //...
```

```
        }, teardown: function() {
          //...
        }
      });

      test("validating empty username", function() {
        //...
      });

      test("validating empty password", function() {
        //...
      });

      test("validating username format", function() {
        //...
      });

      test("validating password format", function() {
        //...
      });
```

After making this change in the QUnit modules, you can now run them safely on the top of the JSTD test runner.

Start the JSTD server as usual, using the following command:

```
java -jar JsTestDriver-1.3.4.b.jar --port 9876
```

Capture two browsers (for example, Firefox and IE) by entering the following URL in the browser's address bar:

```
http://localhost:9876/capture
```

Run the QUnit tests on top of the JSTD test runner, as follows:

```
java -jar JsTestDriver-1.3.4.b.jar --config jsTestDriver-qunit.conf
--tests all --testOutput reports
```

The output in the console will be as follows:

```
Total 24 tests (Passed: 24; Fails: 0; Errors: 0) (1150.00 ms)

Microsoft Internet Explorer 8.0 Windows: Run 12 tests (Passed: 12; Fails:
0; Errors 0) (826.00 ms)

Firefox 15.0.1 Windows: Run 12 tests (Passed: 12; Fails: 0; Errors 0)
(1150.00 ms)
```

In the `reports` folder of the JSTD-QUnit integration, you will find six JUnit XML files (three files for the tests on Firefox and three files for the tests on IE). Every JUnit XML report file contains the test results of a single QUnit module.

Integration with build management tools

Because the JSTD tests can run from the command line, JSTD can be integrated easily with build management tools such as Ant and Maven and also with continuous integration tools such as Hudson. The following code snippet shows an Ant script that runs the `runAllTests.bat` file in the `jstd\tests` folder.

```
<project name="weatherApplication" default="runJSTDTests" basedir=".">
  <target name="runJSTDTests">
    <exec executable="cmd">
      <arg value="/c"/>
      <arg value="runAllTests.bat"/>
    </exec>
  </target>
</project>
```

> For Hudson, you can create a Hudson job that periodically executes the `runAllTests.bat` file as a Windows batch command (if you are working on a Linux environment, you can create a job that periodically executes the Linux shell script file).

As a result of running the tests from the command line, you can also integrate the Jasmine and the QUnit tests, which run on top of the JSTD runner with Ant, Maven, and Hudson.

Thanks to JSTD, we can automate the running of the Jasmine and the QUnit tests and automate the generation of the **test** and **code coverage** reports for these frameworks, which do not have a mechanism provided for integration with the command-line interface.

Integration with the IDEs

In addition to all of the powerful features of JSTD just mentioned, it can also be integrated with different integrated development environments (IDEs) such as **Eclipse** and **IntelliJ**. Thanks to this integration, you can start the JSTD server and run the tests without having to know JSTD commands. Let's see how JSTD can work with Eclipse.

Eclipse integration

In order to work with JSTD on the Eclipse IDE, you need to:

1. Install the JSTD Eclipse plugin.

    i.   In order to install the JSTD plugin in Eclipse, go to **Install new Software** in the **Help** menu.

    ii. Then, add the following installation URL as an update site:

         ```
         http://js-test-driver.googlecode.com/svn/update/
         ```

    iii. Check the **JsTestDriver Plugin for Eclipse** checkbox and click on **Next**. Finally, click on the **Next** button in the **Install details** window, accept any agreements, apply the changes, and restart Eclipse.

2. After installing the JSTD Eclipse plugin, you will need to create a JsTestDriver run configuration by selecting **Run Configurations** from the **Run** menu and then selecting the **Js Test Driver Test** item by right-clicking on it, and clicking on **New**. You will see the JSTD run configuration form as shown in the following screenshot:

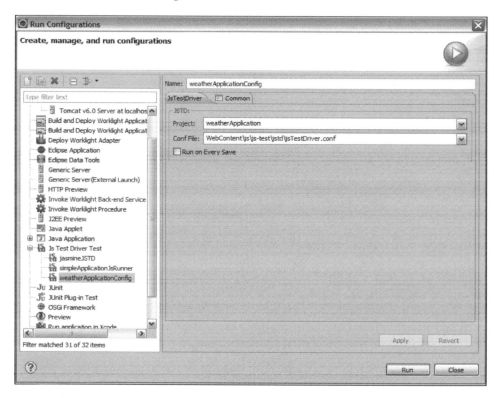

3. In the JSTD run configuration form, you will need to enter the name of the run configuration (`weatherApplicationConfig`), select the web project and the JSTD configuration file, and click on the **Apply** and **Close** buttons. You will then need to start the JSTD server and capture the browsers from the **server panel** as shown in the following screenshot:

4. Using the play and stop buttons in the server panel, you can start and stop the JSTD server. In order to capture one or more browsers, just copy the URL in the server panel and paste in the address bar of the browsers, and they will automatically be captured. Once the browsers are captured, they will be highlighted in the server panel, as shown in the preceding screenshot.

5. Finally, in order to execute the JSTD tests, select **Run Configurations** from the **Run** menu, select the `weatherApplicationConfig` run configuration, and click on the **Run** button. You will see the output of the JSTD test results, as shown in the following screenshot:

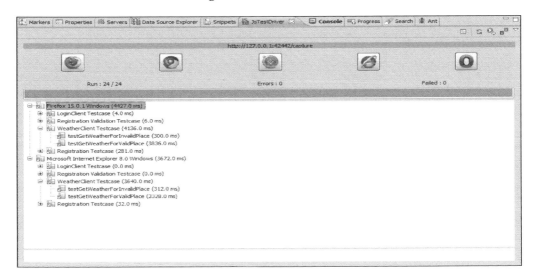

As shown in the preceding screenshot, the server panel displays the test result information, which contains the test name, the test duration, and the browser on which the test is performed.

You can apply these steps again in order to run the Jasmine and QUnit tests (on the top of JSTD) from the Eclipse IDE; the main difference is that you will need to specify the corresponding JSTD test configuration file in the JSTD run configuration form, that is, `jsTestDriver-jasmine.conf` for Jasmine and `jsTestDriver-qunit.conf` for QUnit.

Summary

In this chapter, you learned what JsTestDriver (JSTD) is, the JSTD architecture, the JSTD configuration, and how to use JSTD for testing synchronous JavaScript code. You learned how to test asynchronous (Ajax) JavaScript code using the JSTD `AsyncTestCase` object. You learned the various assertions provided by the framework and how to generate the test and code coverage reports using the framework's code coverage plugin. You also learned how to use JSTD as a test runner for other JavaScript unit testing frameworks, such as Jasmine and QUnit, in order to enable the execution of the tests of these frameworks from the command-line interface. You learned how to integrate the tests of the JSTD (and the tests of the JavaScript frameworks on the top of JSTD) with build and continuous integration tools, such as Ant and Hudson. You learned how to work with the JSTD framework in one of the most popular IDEs, Eclipse.

Index

resume() function 78
testing 78
wait() function 78

B

BasicRunner.html page 102
BDD 31
Behavior-driven development. *See* BDD
boundary testing 35

C

callbacks parameter 145
code coverage 156
configuration file 132
console object 67
Continuous integration (CI) 9
custom Jasmine matchers
  developing 43, 44
custom QUnit assertions
  developing 111, 112

D

datatype assertions 75, 141, 142
deepEqual assertion 109
describe keyword 36
displaySuccessMessage method 24, 28
displayWeatherInformation method 20, 23
DIV element 20
doAjaxOperation method 51

E

Eclipse 167
Eclipse integration, JSTD
  about 168
  working 168-170
equal assertion 109
error callbacks 144
expect assertion 110

F

Factorial Testcase 70
fail() method 77
fail([msg]) assertion 143

G

genhtml command 160
getFactorial method 34
getFactorial test case 71
getWeatherCondition method 20, 23

H

handleRegistrationError method 24, 28
handleWeatherInfoError method 20, 23
HTML code, weather forecasting
    application
  exploring 15
HTML fixtures
  about 51
  jasmine-jquery, configuring 52, 53
  loadFixtures module 53, 54
Hudson
  about 98
  URL 99
Hudson job 99

I

IntelliJ 167
invokeWeatherClient function 20
isInstanceOf assertion 76
isPrimeNumber custom assertion code 112
isTypeOf() method 76

J

Jasmine
  about 31
  configuring 31, 32
  download link 31
  test, writing 32-38
JasmineAdapter.js file
  URL 162
jasmine-jquery plugin
  configuring 52, 53
Jasmine matchers
  about 39
  toBe 39, 40
  toBeDefined 40
  toBeFalsy 41

Thank you for buying
JavaScript Unit Testing

About Packt Publishing

Packt, pronounced 'packed', published its first book "*Mastering phpMyAdmin for Effective MySQL Management*" in April 2004 and subsequently continued to specialize in publishing highly focused books on specific technologies and solutions.

Our books and publications share the experiences of your fellow IT professionals in adapting and customizing today's systems, applications, and frameworks. Our solution based books give you the knowledge and power to customize the software and technologies you're using to get the job done. Packt books are more specific and less general than the IT books you have seen in the past. Our unique business model allows us to bring you more focused information, giving you more of what you need to know, and less of what you don't.

Packt is a modern, yet unique publishing company, which focuses on producing quality, cutting-edge books for communities of developers, administrators, and newbies alike. For more information, please visit our website: www.packtpub.com.

About Packt Open Source

In 2010, Packt launched two new brands, Packt Open Source and Packt Enterprise, in order to continue its focus on specialization. This book is part of the Packt Open Source brand, home to books published on software built around Open Source licences, and offering information to anybody from advanced developers to budding web designers. The Open Source brand also runs Packt's Open Source Royalty Scheme, by which Packt gives a royalty to each Open Source project about whose software a book is sold.

Writing for Packt

We welcome all inquiries from people who are interested in authoring. Book proposals should be sent to author@packtpub.com. If your book idea is still at an early stage and you would like to discuss it first before writing a formal book proposal, contact us; one of our commissioning editors will get in touch with you.

We're not just looking for published authors; if you have strong technical skills but no writing experience, our experienced editors can help you develop a writing career, or simply get some additional reward for your expertise.

open source
community experience distilled

JavaScript Testing Beginner's Guide

ISBN: 978-1-849510-00-4   Paperback: 272 pages

Test and debug JavaScript the easy way

1. Learn different techniques to test JavaScript, no matter how long or short your code might be.

2. Discover the most important and free tools to help make your debugging task less painful.

3. Discover how to test user interfaces that are controlled by JavaScript.

4. Make use of free built-in browser features to quickly find out why your JavaScript code is not working, and most importantly, how to debug it.

Object-Oriented JavaScript

ISBN: 978-1-847194-14-5   Paperback: 356 pages

Create scalable, reusable high-quality JavaScript applications, and libraries

1. Learn to think in JavaScript, the language of the web browser

2. Object-oriented programming made accessible and understandable to web developers

3. Do it yourself: experiment with examples that can be used in your own scripts

Please check **www.PacktPub.com** for information on our titles

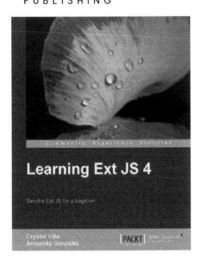

[PACKT] open source
community experience distilled

PUBLISHING

Learning Ext JS 4

ISBN: 978-1-849516-84-6   Paperback: 504 pages

Sencha Ext JS for a beginner

1. Learn the basics and create your first classes

2. Handle data and understand the way it works, create powerful widgets and new components

3. Dig into the new architecture defined by Sencha and work on real world projects

Appcelerator Titanium: Patterns and Best Practices

ISBN: 978-1-849693-48-6   Paperback: 120 pages

Take your Titanium development experience to the next level, and build your Titanium knowledge on CommonJS structuring, MVC model implementation, memory management and much more

1. Full step-by-step approach to help structure your apps in an MVC style that will make them more maintainable, easier to code and more stable

2. Learn best practices and optimizations both related directly to JavaScript and Titanium itself

3. Learn solutions to create cross-compatible layouts that work across both Android and the iPhone and utilize the new Appcelerator Cloud Services to bring your apps to the market faster than every before

Please check **www.PacktPub.com** for information on our titles

Made in the USA
Lexington, KY
19 July 2013